The Big Book
of Presbyterian Stewardship

The Big Book
of Presbyterian Stewardship

Elaine W. Barnett
Laura S. Gordon
Margaret A. Hendrix

Geneva Press
Louisville, Kentucky

Book design by Sharon Adams
Cover design by Rohani Design

First Edition
Published by Geneva Press
Louisville, Kentucky

This book is printed on acid-free paper that meets the American National Standards Institute Z39.48 standard. ∞

PRINTED IN THE UNITED STATES OF AMERICA
01 02 03 04 05 06 07 08 09 10 — 10 9 8 7 6 5 4 3 2 1

Library of Congress Cataloging-in-Publication Data

Barnett, Elaine W., 1944–
   The big book of Presbyterian stewardship / Elaine W. Barnett, Laura S. Gordon, Margaret A. Hendrix.—1st ed.
      p. cm.
   Includes bibliographical references.
   ISBN 0-664-50157-5 (alk. paper)
      1. Presbyterian Church—Finance. 2. Church finance. I. Gordon, Laura S., 1940– II. Hendrix, Margaret A., 1944– III. Title.

BX9189.5 B37 2000
254'.8'088251—dc21   00-041720

CONTENTS

QUOTATIONS ABOUT STEWARDSHIP

Much has been written and spoken about stewardship—about the joy that comes from generous giving and the responsibility that each Christian has to give back some measure of the gifts that God has given. Here are some particularly thought-provoking quotes by noted authors.

As long as our civilization is essentially one of property, of fences, of exclusiveness, it will be mocked by delusions. Our riches will leave us sick, there will be bitterness in our laughter, and our wine will burn our mouth. Only that good profits which we can taste with all doors open and which serve all [men]. Ralph Waldo Emerson

We live in a world where it is estimated that thirty-five thousand children under the age of five die daily around the globe, most from preventable poverty conditions and many in areas where no church has been planted to tell them of Jesus' love. We can be confident that such conditions are not God's will: Perhaps one idea that would not be debatable in any part of the church is that Jesus loves the little children of the world. The financial cost to end most of these child deaths, it has been proposed, is about $2.5 billion a year, which is the amount Americans spend on chewing gum. *Behind the Stained Glass Windows*, p. 218

You are Christian only . . . so long as you constantly pose critical questions to the society you live in, so long as you emphasize the need of conversion both for yourself and for the world, . . . so long as you stay unsatisfied with the status quo and keep saying that a new world is yet to come. You are a Christian only when you believe you have a role to play in the realization of this new Kingdom, and when you urge everyone you meet with holy unrest to make haste so that the promise might soon be fulfilled. *Circles of Love* by Henri Nouwen; Darton, Longman, & Todd, 1988

The front lines may lie within our own congregations. The issues need to be identified in order to be clearly faced. Without a clear theological framework or constructive use for money that focuses the congregation outward, congregations have turned inward. One side effect is the resulting utter-control dynamics that define the missions of many congregations. *Behind the Stained Glass Windows*, p. 219

In the long run it is only to the [man] of morality that wealth comes. We believe in the harmony of God's Universe. We know that it is only by working along His laws natural and spiritual that we can work with efficiency. Only by working along the lines of right thinking and right living can the secrets of wealth of nature be revealed. . . . Godliness is in league with riches. . . . Material prosperity is helping to make the national character sweeter, more joyous, more unselfish, more Christianlike. That is my answer to the question as to the relation of material prosperity to morality. William Lawrence, Episcopal Bishop of Massachusetts

STEWARDSHIP TIPS

Some people might call this a page filler! But we believe these are important stewardship tips related to the importance of shared leadership between the pastor and church leaders and the development of a sense of openness in all areas of stewardship. Did you know that . . .

✔ *If* pastors preached the same percentage of sermons on stewardship as Jesus told parables on money and stewardship, we would hear seventeen sermons on stewardship each year? How many sermons do you hear on stewardship? How many sermons do you preach on stewardship?

> See **Tool #8** in the Toolbox Section for some ideas.
> Have a Bible study time at a session meeting looking for those stewardship references by Jesus.

✔ *If* pastors and church leaders were more open about their own giving and stewardship, the congregation would be encouraged to become more open and more generous givers? Thus, as pastor, let the congregation know how much is given to the mission and ministry of your congregation by the team of clergy and lay leaders. Ordinarily the pastor and the pastor's family are among the top five givers in a congregation. And everyone knows exactly what the pastor earns. The clergy and lay team members should communicate with humility their generous spirit and sincere gratitude.

✔ *If* congregations were able to adopt an open attitude about giving, people could be helped to be more faithful stewards? There would be an increase in giving to the congregation through the annual giving and a variety of planned giving programs. People often believe that the amount of money individuals give should be a BIG secret. More and more church leaders are realizing their responsibility to help people grow in their giving level.

Those people with this insight have challenged others by saying, "If the rest of a person's spiritual life were out of step, you'd go and talk with him or her. Why do we shy away from open conversation about money?"

Steps to begin this level of openness:

1. The pastor is open about the personal giving of his or her family.
2. The Stewardship Committee members are willing to be open with the congregation about their giving.
3. The Stewardship Committee has access to the giving level of members and friends in the congregation.
4. Many people rotate on and off the Stewardship Committee.

INTRODUCTION

In their book *Behind the Stained Glass Windows: Money Dynamics in the Church*, John and Sylvia Ronsvalle make the observation that the lack of a positive agenda in the church contributes to making money a confusing entity. They believe that in most cases neither denominations nor individual congregations, let alone their intermediate governing bodies, have what they call a "commonly acknowledged, overarching vision." Without this commonly held vision, people are not sure their money is needed. When the church is confused about its purpose, it cannot help people make constructive use of their money. Because of a lack of broad mission commitment, giving to the local congregation actually works out to be giving to ourselves. This situation is one reason why building campaigns may be used as a rallying point—they provide a purpose (p. 211).

In this book, the writers hope to stimulate your thinking about how we earn our money, what we believe about work and money, and, therefore, how and why we spend our money, and specifically how we view giving to God through the church. We hope that clergy and lay church leaders will learn some new tools to develop a "commonly acknowledged, overarching vision," develop a year-round stewardship program, and increase the spirituality of members through their giving. It is essential that the pastor and all committees in the congregation that are related to stewardship and giving study this book simultaneously.

We will explore the connection between various theories about motivations for giving. Judith Nichols, author of numerous books on fund-raising in the not-for-profit area, believes the tithe is a limiting and inappropriate factor. She believes each entity must know its target population and know what people might be capable of giving. Money must be requested in specific ways that touch givers and "pull their heart strings" so that they are confident that the gifts they give are going to make the world a better place. Providing accountability creates for the giver a sense that something good has been done. Nichols believes accountability is vital in today's world.

Another area of concern is the need to understand the different generational markers that give clues regarding how people of different generations think about money and giving. Understanding these markers will direct the way in which messages about giving are delivered to different age groups and suggest how much money should be asked for in any given circumstance. The basis of information in this area comes from the work of William Strauss and Neil Howe in their book *Generations*, which is also used by Nichols.

Finally, but most important, the giver must give because giving is part of spiritual health and well-being. People must be helped to understand that collecting possessions—consuming—does not bring happiness or self-esteem. The great spiritual hole people feel in their lives—the cry for spiritual development (whatever that means)—is directly connected to the dryness that results in greed and consumption, and the church is not addressing these issues as a prophetic voice.

Because giving and spiritual health and well-being are directly connected, it is imperative that pastors and key church leaders know how much money members are giving. If we really believe that giving and spiritual growth are connected, then the team of pastor and lay leaders must know about giving because they are the ones to lead the development. The Ronsvalles state that, "in a church there are only growing or non-growing Christians. When you talk about human expectations, you are introducing unspoken rules. The goal should be the spiritual growth of the individual, not raising a budget" (p. 200).

In this book, we will acquaint church leaders with resources and information available from a variety of sources. There are much new data, research, and theories about giving that are available from religious and secular sources. This book collects under one cover helpful resources and information for the pastor and session as the members design and implement a plan of stewardship. This plan is faithful to the gospel and effective in accomplishing the mission of the church, and it encourages a deeper personal relationship with God through giving.

We have attended many conferences, heard many speakers, and done much reading in the area of stewardship. We have tried to quote all our sources when their ideas and thoughts were used. If we have failed to give proper credit, we ask forgiveness, for we owe a debt of gratitude to all the workshop leaders, pastors, and authors who have helped us on our stewardship journeys.

The purpose of this book is to . . .

- Understand the forces and factors that determine how people make decisions about the use of money and how spending choices are made.

- Provide resources for congregations to formulate a realistic picture of their giving potential. This book includes tools to assess the congregation's financial base, identify who its members are, implement a program to increase giving, and maintain the program.

- Design an effective stewardship program that articulates the vision of the church in a way that speaks to members and friends of the congregation.

SUGGESTED STEPS TO OPTIMIZE THE USE OF THIS BOOK

Step One: Ask the pastor/session to assign this book to appropriate committees for study.

Step Two: Read the first four chapters, which are designed to deepen knowledge and broaden thinking about the ways money influences our culture and our culture influences our use of money.

Step Three: Complete the assessment tools as they are mentioned in the various chapters.

Step Four: Complete the exercises at the ends of various chapters. It is critical that ample consideration be given Chapters One through Four because they concern the crux of stewardship issues in the postmodern church.

Step Five: Read the case study in Chapter Ten to use as a guide for significant benchmarks as you consider the stewardship and giving history and future of your congregation.

Step Six: Read Chapters Five through Nine. Complete the appropriate study guides.

Step Seven: Complete the assessment tools # 1–3 in the Toolbox.

Step Eight: Read Chapters Ten and Eleven and complete the exercises at the end of each of them.

MORE STEWARDSHIP TIPS
ABOUT ASKING FOR MONEY

✔ Experts say, "Ask for four times as much money as you think a person can give." You'll be surprised at the results.

✔ Offer the opportunity to give over a longer period. "Can't give $500? How about giving $200 a quarter? " Often that suggestion leads to a larger total contribution.

✔ Be willing to share what your financial commitment is to the project in a way that indicates why you feel the money will be used in ways compatible with the mission priorities.

✔ The Stewardship and Finance Committees and the session will benefit from a study of a book like Jouette Bassler's *God and Mammon—Asking for Money in the New Testament*, or Sondra Wheeler's *Wealth as Peril and Obligation—The New Testament on Possessions.*

✔ If you don't ask for money, you won't receive any.

Chapter 1

UNDERSTANDING THE INFLUENCES OF SOCIETY

Consumerism—Work—Money

If I am hungry it is a material problem. If someone else is hungry it is a spiritual problem.
Nicholas Berdyaev

The Protestant work ethic has provided Americans with a religious basis for work and for the use of time and wealth. This ethic may be defined as placing as priority in one's daily life behavior that encouraged industriousness, thrifty living, and careful management of material things. This ethic has changed its emphasis according to the needs of the current economic understanding. These changes include revisions of religious imperatives to accommodate the changing economic desires of the present society. Whatever the "truth" about the Protestant work ethic has been for any individual, it is important to realize that work and wealth have been the backbone of American lifestyle and carry with them both good and evil, reality and myth.

To understand what motivates people to give their money to the church or to charity is vital. One must reach into history and begin with the meaning of work—or that which produces money or wealth for most people in American society today.

- For Greeks and Romans, work was to be avoided by the elite and left to slaves. Philosophers and soldiers were honored.

- The Hebrews saw work as "painful drudgery" to which [man] is condemned by sin. The Hebrews looked on work as atonement for original sin.

- For Christians, work is introduced in the Bible as part of the creation narrative. God is first known in the work of creation, and labor is portrayed as a normal condition of life for humans because of the original sin of Adam and Eve.

- In early Christianity and through the Middle Ages, the one reason for amassing wealth was to dispense charity. There was disdain not only for work, but for interest, usury, and profit.

• By the end of the Middle Ages, work was a wearisome and painful pursuit. It was the mark of [men] trapped by necessity and not wholly free.

THE GREAT SPLIT

Along came the Reformation, which sanctified all work and destroyed past negative views of work. It made work ethical and honorable. Profit-seeking became respectable. The Reformation brought work in line with the needs of the economy and carried strong messages about the individual in relation to the universe, work, and wealth. "This is quite a different perspective from that of biblical faith which sees work as having no meaning in itself. It has value only insofar as it contributes to God's purposes in creation and community" (Owensby, 52).

THE GREAT SPLIT BETWEEN RELIGIOUS
PIETY AND WORLDLY ACTIVITY RESOLVED

Luther established the idea that salvation could come only through God's grace, not through work. He believed that work was natural to fallen humanity and that idleness was an unnatural and evil evasion. Working to maintain oneself was a way of serving God, but it did not buy salvation. With this idea, the great split between religious piety and worldly activity was resolved; profession becomes "calling," and work is valued as a religious path to salvation.

PROFIT-MAKING IS SANCTIFIED

• For centuries, Christianity had condemned profit-making.

• With the Reformation and Calvin, accumulation of wealth was taken as a sign that one was among God's elect.

• Cotton Mather, Puritan leader and pastor, took this notion further to make all work that supported or enhanced the community a "calling" and went on to purport that slothfulness would bring poverty, misery, and confusion.

Years later, John Wesley pointed out that religion would produce industry and frugality, which would lead to riches. As riches increased, so would pride, anger, and desire. In this way, religion would bring on its own decay.

PROFIT-MAKING AND RELIGION SEPARATED

• Mather further set up a paradox that has allowed people to separate what they do in their work or "calling" from how they see their actions in their religious lives.

• Mather taught that the general calling of each person should not swallow up the personal calling because personal devotion to God was to come first.

- Through his sermons and teaching, Mather deserves recognition as one of the first to teach that American business [men] could serve God through making money—that godliness is equated with riches.
- He taught that it is God who controls our fortune, but by thought, word, and deed, we can influence God to exercise control in our favor. At the same time, Mather taught that material things can corrupt the soul. No matter what our worldly success, our treasures in heaven measure our highest success.

The result of Mather's influence, and the development of what became known as the Protestant work ethic, brought hope for a better future for the common person for the first time in the history of the world. It meant that God had made provision for all persons to succeed.

PROTESTANT WORK ETHIC BECOMES A GOSPEL OF WORLDLY SUCCESS

- Benjamin Franklin took the position that wealth was the result of virtue.
- Franklin's writings persuade the reader that character and success are related as cause and effect. He argued that our destiny is in our own hands because each is able to develop his or her own character, and good character brings good reward.
- The biblical image of calling is radically changed by Franklin. It is reason, not God, that calls persons to labor for common good.
- This world rather than the next was Franklin's central concern. Work was a societal necessity and a means for improving one's station in life, but it was done on the fulfillment of divine commandment. Virtue became the means to a good life.

Franklin helped to make the shift from the piety of the Puritan to the moralism of the nineteenth century. Both Mather and Franklin agreed that cultivating certain virtues led to wealth, but Mather justified it primarily as a way of worshiping God. Franklin also justified it as a means to a final end, but an end less concerned with religious implications. These ends were the leisure that money provided to enable people to do what they wanted in life. The end result was that any persons without religious convictions could make money and still consider themselves virtuous.

RAGS TO RICHES AND THE SUCCESS LITERATURE

- With the success literature and the ideas of people like Horatio Alger and Andrew Carnegie, Franklin was idolized as the epitome of success.
- "Getting ahead" was now based on individual effort and luck.
- The Puritans had believed that people were born into a fixed social sphere and that ambition or the desire to leave one's appointed station in life was sinful. Franklin, on the other hand, encouraged the wish to advance in the

social hierarchy. By standing on their own, working hard, being virtuous, and having a little bit of luck, people would be successful.

WORK, MONEY, AND THE INFLUENCE OF ADAM SMITH

- Smith believed that the individual acting in his or her own interests would do that which would also be in the best interest of all.

- Smith claimed that labor was the ultimate source of wealth. It created a system without a soul. Economic progress would bring many benefits and would lead to the establishment of rational religion, founded on the commercial principle of free competition.

- Smith believed that commodity consumption and the status that expensive symbols bring make people excessively ambitious, which causes them to lose their peace of mind.

- Smith insisted that a person's character is the result, not the cause, of the way his [or her] living is earned; in the same way, a nation's character is the product of the most common form of economic activity practiced in that nation.

- Smith went on to say that for the most part, work was not enjoyable and that it was in everyone's best interest to have as much leisure as possible. He believed that [men] do work, but that they work to consume. He suggested that consumption is the sole end and purpose of all production, that job satisfaction is rare, and that most people work for money.

- Smith felt that the desire for consumer goods could never be satisfied, that consumer goods might begin to be worshiped for their own sake, and that peace would be disrupted.

MAKING MONEY AS THE CENTRAL GOAL OF AMERICAN SOCIETY

- By the nineteenth century, making money was people's central goal. Everything had its price.

- Success writers like Andrew Carnegie promoted two types of success: The first was money; the second was true success, which was happiness, joy in living, developing oneself by doing one's best, leading a self-respecting life, and peace of mind. The focus was on self.

- Success was about getting money and then feeling good about oneself. Service and good for the community were incidental for the most part. This clash between materialism and idealism in the American spirit created a deeper need to justify success.

- The success writers justified the accumulation of wealth as the socially, morally, and economically right thing to do. Patriotism was invoked because accumulating wealth helped to build the nation.

- The accumulation of wealth had always been supported as the outgrowth of American opportunity.

- The free individual in a democratic society and the acceptance of wealth and its status for the wealthy person set the stage for consumption.

RELIGIOUS LEADERS SUPPORT THE ACCUMULATION OF WEALTH

- Many religious leaders found it necessary to qualify their praise of big business and its leaders. They reconciled private gain and Christianity.

- Leaders preached the old doctrine of the rich [man] as the steward or trustee, obligated to use [his] wealth for the glory of God or for the welfare of humankind.

- Service to humanity was touted as the one justification for the possession of great wealth. From the above concepts, men like Andrew Carnegie and the captains of industry found a justification for their wealth.

THE INDUSTRIAL REVOLUTION

So much of the ethos of the early days of American society was centered in its agrarian life. The frontier and the farm communities had provided income, community, and a sense of worth to the majority of Americans. Manufacturing had been done in homes and small shops, by hand. Each artisan took pride in the craft or trade and in the finished product.

The Industrial Revolution brought massive changes in the working lives of Americans. Manufacturing now took place in factories. Workers often produced only one part of a product and rarely experienced pride in the finished product. More items were produced than could be consumed.

FROM "CALLING" TO SOCIAL DUTY TO PRODUCE

- The nation had begun with its values about work based on spiritual necessities. The Protestant faith was the national basis for understanding economic life.

- Early in American life, accumulating wealth, whether it was property or money, became central. We know that for the first time in history, work was deemed worthwhile.

- To move from the rural economic system to the factory economic system, the Industrial Revolution needed the Protestant work ethic standards based on diligence, hard work, frugality, and scarcity.

- To buy the mass-produced goods, consumption had to be increased.

MOVEMENT TO URBAN CENTERS

With the Industrial Revolution, thousands came to the urban centers—the new frontiers. The western frontier had closed at just about the time the Industrial Revolution got underway. As people moved to this new frontier—for the same reasons they had moved west (to better themselves)—they did not find the sense of community in the same way that they had in more rural settings. Rather than finding security in community as in the past, workers began to try to reduce their anxiety by the accumulation of wealth and material comforts.

- The central premise of the work ethic was that work was the core of moral life. Gradually, the term "calling" faded from common speech and with it the idea that one labored for the glory of God.

- Nineteenth-century Americans were told by factory owners and entrepreneurs that in a world of pressing material needs, it was one's social duty to produce. Each individual was dependent on his or her self to move up the ladder of success.

ROLE CHANGES

In agrarian America, every man, woman, and child knew their role. They knew how their contributions fitted into the needs of the family and the community. Each knew that the rest could not fully exist without them. In an economic system with long apprenticeships, pride was felt in the product. Products were made for individuals, and the relationship between craftsman and individual purchaser essentially affected the definition of work.

LOSS OF IDENTITY AND SELF-ESTEEM

- When the move to the urban centers and factories came, that sense of identity and purpose and that sense of community and pride in work faded. The factory worker was now just one "cog in the wheel" who did not necessarily understand or know the purpose of the tasks of the other workers or have pride in the product.

- Work was often just drudgery. In a situation where a person's job had decreasing significance for the broad issue of social survival, wages emerged as the clearest connection between the individual worker and the issue of survival.

- As mass production and standardization became more common, the worker had to do the same operations over and over again. The lack of skill required in this process minimized pride in accomplishment.

- Laborers whose self-esteem had previously depended on their ability as artisans or farmers found little fulfillment in their new status as a "machine's helper." The result was boredom, frustration, and anger.

- The value of industriousness was lost. The unique American opportunity to earn bountiful rewards for increased effort was turned upside down.

- Industrialization eventually eroded the certainty that work would bring success to the individual. The resulting negative feelings toward work brought demands for more and more economic compensation in exchange for surrendering to such meaningless activity. The labor movement came along to rescue the worker.

RESPONSE OF THE PROTESTANT LEADERS

Meanwhile, Protestant leaders denounced the labor movement, suggesting that the eight-hour workday would produce too much leisure, which would lead to an increase in vice. The poor, it was suggested, should be content with their wages and with the understanding that in the Lord's good time, they would get more if they deserved it. Church leaders continued to believe that the nation was sound. They believed that greed at the top could be ignored or accepted as a tool of progress. Misery at the bottom could be waved aside as inevitable or, at most, treated by a program of guarded and labeled philanthropy. A large part of Protestantism still believed in the old axioms of hard work and self-help and rejected the social teachings of Christianity on moral and economic grounds.

VIRTUE SHIFTS FROM PRODUCTION TO CONSUMPTION

By the 1920s, businessmen feared that labor revolts could lead to bolshevism. Big business leaders felt that mass production, leading to mass consumption, would be the answer to labor's unrest. The logical step was to manage workers' lives by promoting consumption as the answer to the unhappiness created by the factory and the unsatisfying workplace. It is at this point that virtue shifts from production to consumption.

EXCESSIVENESS REPLACES THRIFT

The worker had to be changed into a consumer as well as a producer. New habits and concepts of success had to be created. The whole population, not just the elite, must become the market if sales were to keep up with mass production. Excessiveness would have to replace thrift as a social value. Adam Smith had already laid the foundation for the consumer society. He had described consumption as a social action or an attempt by each person to acquire the symbols needed to identify status. All the virtues of scarcity had been outmoded by the new consumer society.

IMMEDIATE GRATIFICATION PROMOTED

The central task of those producing and selling products became to create new wants and new desires. An issue of *The Journal of Retailing* in the mid-1950s quotes marketing consultant Victor Lebrow's proposed plea for forced consumption:

> Our enormously productive economy . . . demands that we make consumption our way of life, that we convert the buying and use of goods into rituals, that we seek our spiritual satisfaction, our ego satisfaction,

in consumption. . . . We need things consumed, burned up, worn out, replaced, and discarded at an ever increasing rate. (Lebrow)

The ethic of frugality and scarcity was out the window, and the ethic of immediate gratification was the order of the day. The worker now worked to have money to buy things to bring happiness, spiritual fulfillment, and self-esteem.

CONSUMPTION AS ADDICTION

It is no wonder that Americans have succumbed to the lure of consumption. The anxieties, lack of fulfillment, loss of community, lack of individual contribution, and sense of longing have led the average American to seek his or her afterlife in the shopping center.

- Friendship, intimacy, love, pride, happiness, and joy are actually the objects we buy and consume. Because none of these deepest human hopes can be fulfilled in any product, the mere consumption of them is never enough.

- Consumption emerges as a way of life—as an addiction.

- Americans have been led from a culture of hard work, discipline, and self-denial to a culture of consumption that is centered in waste and immediate gratification.

- Consumption and waste are now considered a duty.

- This is a radical change from early American society where work for production was considered a duty, a contribution to the community and to the glory of God!

WORK AND IDENTITY LINKED

- In our society, work has always had the function of supplying identity.

- One's work indicated the kind of person he or she was and the position he or she held in life.

- Work was a basis for belonging in the community.

- When people spend less time working and work in mindless jobs that feel useless or harmful, what happens to the sense of identity?

It can be said that much of society's ills today are based on our lifestyles that are rooted in the consumer society.

We have learned to consume everything around us, to use it up, to throw it away if it does not work right or if we lose interest in it, and to measure our worth and dignity by the amount of goods and services we can consume and own. Our success is based on our possessions. We consume not only goods and services, but relationships, organizations, and, yes, even our churches. We long for community, for support, for a sense of belonging and security, and we wonder why we cannot find it.

NEW THINGS ARE HAPPENING

- The beginning of the twenty-first century has found Americans ensnared in the Information Revolution.

- Fewer people earn their income in factory or agrarian pursuits.

- In the agrarian society and on the frontier, people needed one another to survive.

- In the industrial society, people seemed to need one another less—each can do his or her own task independent of others, without concern for the whole.

- The Information Revolution suggests connections and need, but isolates people even further. Workers can do their job at home, dress as they please, and choose their own hours. Leisure is often spent at the computer instead of engaged in activities with other persons.

LOSS OF SPIRITUALITY

The cry so often heard now for spirituality in people's lives is a direct result of the hollowness that consumption creates. We were conditioned to satisfy our longings through consumption, and it has let us down. Our society takes our deepest longings and feelings (love, sex, acceptance, and purpose) and attempts to transfer them into commodities to be exploited for profit. We have lost our religious base for work and production.

Some Americans are starting to think that the time has passed for unending affluence and consumption as a way of life. Finding hope and fulfillment in consumerism may have had its day. It may have been realized that possessions have the tendency to possess the possessors. People become slaves to their wealth. Affluence has not meant the liberation of human creativity, but it has meant a new form of slavery. People have demanded ever new products, but have accepted constant dullness and boredom.

TIME FOR A NEW AMERICAN WORK ETHIC

Work has taken on many faces over the years. It has changed in its understanding from being a curse that only slaves were required to do, to being an act of immense value in a shared community setting, an act to the glory of God. It has been a source of freedom of expression and creativity and of individuality. It has been a source of servitude and mindless, boring, routine, and backbreaking activity. It has been an activity for the sustenance of life and the building up of the whole; and it has been the way one spent the least amount of time to earn the most money so that happiness could be sought in leisure, consumption, spiritual fulfillment, and self-esteem.

For a new American work ethic to take shape and form, the meaning of work may well become the meaning of life itself. It is becoming clear that Americans want to work at jobs that have meaning and that do some good for humankind. They want jobs that emphasize personal creativity, self-expression, personal relationships, harmony with nature, the search for the sacred, and the satisfaction that comes with exploring the full richness of human experience. These are the ingredients for a newer and stronger work ethic.

People may expect to work to provide themselves with personal fulfillment, social relationships, and connection to the community just as they did in our early history. One could say that work should not be primarily a thing one does to live, but a thing one lives to do and the medium by which the worker offers himself or herself to God.

To make the information in this chapter have more relevance for your congregation, ask individual committee members to think about their family history as far back as they can remember. Then ask them to answer the following questions:

1. What did your family say and do about money?
2. How was money earned?
3. How was money spent?

Chapter 2

GENERATIONS AND MONEY

But to what will I compare this generation?
Matthew 11:16

Every church is concerned about money in one way or another—either about how to raise the operating and mission budget or about how to build a new building or repair the old one. Almost no church can say, "We have all the money we need." Certainly, very few churches tithe beyond their own needs, and even fewer Presbyterians tithe.

We have reached a point in our corporate Presbyterian lives where we need to ask what we must do to change the situation. We have excellent theological tools, resources, training, and preaching about stewardship. We need to hone our skills in these areas and add some tools to our resource bank. We need to learn some of the sociological factors and secular fund-raising techniques and translate them into the religious realm.

We now are going to examine what is known as the role of psychographics, which includes the study of demographics as well as sociological and psychological factors. Combined and analyzed, these factors can help determine what makes people buy certain items, join particular groups, give to one charity or another, and even join a certain church and give time and money to that church. Psychographics is a marketing tool. It is a tool we in the church need to know about and apply, where appropriate, to our stewardship programs.

Generations, written in 1991 by William Strauss and Neil Howe, has become a landmark document to understanding today's and tomorrow's societies. Few of us understand how age groups and generations differ, but the differences are profound, and we encounter them daily. Each generation has its own personality, and the personalities are arranged in a generational constellation that changes according to a predictable generational cycle. Projecting the cycle is a new way to predict attitudes and lifestyles.

Understanding these generational constellations and their personalities is vital to understanding what motivates people to give their money, in what form they give it, and to what causes. It also informs our understanding of how persons of different generations interact in groups and in decision-making situations and what aspects of the church's mission are engaging to them.

The authors of *Generations* tell us that eighteen generations, each roughly twenty to twenty-five birth years in length, have lived on American soil since the 1620s. Seven are still alive today, and two of these are very old. The five younger generations form what is called the "generational constellation" of 1998 (this constellation will remain in effect until most of the oldest one has died and a new one begins about 2003). Strauss and Howe do not look at generations as age brackets that allow us to move from one generation to another, but as a generational diagonal. The basis for the differences in generations arises from how they were raised as children, what public events they witnessed in adolescence, and what social mission their elders gave them as they came of age.

According to Strauss and Howe, the current generational constellation lines up like this:

G.I. (Civic) Generation born 1901 to 1924. They developed a special and good-kid reputation. They were protected by child labor laws, benefited from the development of vitamins, and were given new opportunities such as scouting clubs and new playgrounds. More G.I. children benefited from schooling than any other children at any time in the past. As children and young adults they endured the Depression and World War I. In midlife, often subsidized by the G.I. Bill, they developed sprawling suburbs, discovered new technology, enjoyed new types of entertainment in the form of movies and television, and invented medical miracles like vaccines and other diagnostic tools. They experienced the Arms Race and all the development related to it—they even put a man on the moon! Their generation saw the advent of Social Security and Medicare. They were the generation of problem-solvers, confident and rational. They were a generation of engineers, architects, and builders. They always knew how to get the big jobs done and to do them together. As mature citizens, they have boundless civic optimism. They support institutions, like the church, because it is the "right thing" to do. They trust the will of the community and put their trust in authority and government. They pass on their values of stewardship. They believe in endowments.

SILENT (Adaptive) Generation born 1925 to 1942. They were the restrained children of the Depression and war. They were part of the conformist generation of the "Lonely Crowd." They took no chances; they did what was expected of them and sought job security by working for big companies to whom they were loyal. They believe that fair process is more important than final results when dealing with people, relationships, and conflict. Now they are the litigators, arbitrators, technocrats, and reconcilers of the multicultural society they have helped to make more complex. They were the youngest-marrying generation in American history and often came from divorced parents of multichild households. They were the rock and rollers of the 1950s, participants in the civil rights movement, and volunteers for Kennedy's Peace Corps.

The Silent generation relies on groups to provide direction and purpose. Group therapy, talk shows, think-tanks, buzz groups, committees, and interest groups provide a way for everyone to have their say and be heard. They have fueled the most prosperous generation in history and have become expert consumers, but they lack a sense of purpose. They rely on dietary aids, exercise classes, cosmetic surgery, hair replacement, relaxation therapies, and psychiatric treatments. They live with a vague sense of dissatisfaction with jobs, families, their children, and themselves. As they enter elderhood, they become more adventurous, enjoy their unprecedented affluence, but remain undecided.

BOOM (Idealist) Generation born 1943 to 1960: According to Strauss and Howe in *American Demographics* (April 1991), Boomers were heirs to a national triumph in World War II, born into an era of optimism, arrogance, and affluence. The influence of Dr. Spock and the permissiveness he promoted was balanced by the conformism of the 1950's life in the suburbs. Family life was modeled by *Beaver Cleaver* friendliness and *Father Knows Best* morality. Boomers came of age rebelling against the ideal of their parents. They became flower-child hippies and draft resisters. The flower children and drug culture were out to make the world a better, more self-aware place to live. They have tended to ignore anything that did not "meet their needs" all the while becoming America's greatest consumer generation. Boomers are intense individualists and have a hard time arriving at a consensus and mobilizing to get things done as a group. "Boomers are marked by a weak instinct for social discipline combined with a desire to infuse new values into the institutions they are inheriting. In all spheres of life, they display a bent toward inner absorption, perfectionism and individual self-esteem" (*American Demographics* 27). After having lived through the 1960s and the moral decay that they believed the Silent generation allowed, they now want to set the nation's moral agenda. Boomers will donate their money if they believe the cause can make the world a better place and can show them accountability. They want to know that their money is being spent as directed.

13th (Reactive) Generation born 1961 to 1981: This generation is the thirteenth one to call themselves American citizens. Also known as Generation X, they are the babies of the 1960s and 1970s. They have grown up with a sense of rejection and alienation, children of divorced parents who almost always worked outside the home. They are the first generation of Americans who do not see their economic future as being brighter than that of their parents. As college students they were criticized as dumb and had to work their way through the maze of sexually transmitted diseases and AIDs. They sense little social approval for their generation and express that through body piercing, rap music, and dressing down.

13ers date and marry cautiously. In their jobs, they have little loyalty to corporations and seek more risky avenues for making their money. They are not interested in meetings or planning sessions. They are even less interested in group therapy and action groups. If there is something to be done, they just want to get busy and do it. They will not be good committee members in our churches, nor will they put up with long debates. They will not give to the institution, per se, but they will give to programs like Habitat for Humanity, which promises to make the world a better place. When 13ers have children, they dote on them. They are willing to have less family income in order for one parent to be able to stay at home with the children. They want church and community programs that meet the needs of their children.

MILLENNIAL (Civic) Generation born 1982 to 2003: They are the stars of cuddly-baby movies and commercials, and national leaders have targeted them as a smarter, better-behaving, and more civic-spirited wave of American youth than ever before. Family values, the two-parent family, child abuse, child safety, and education have become key issues for parents of Millennial children. Bookstores are filled with books on how to raise smart, well-behaved, value-centered children. Movies have cute, cheerful, smart children instead of devil worshipers and bad seeds. Millennial children are being raised with delicate hands and a sense of value and virtue. Boomers want to set the moral agenda to aid these tots on their life journey. Magnet schools, private schools, school uniforms, and massive numbers of sporting and cultural activities are accessible to these young Americans. They very likely will grow up generous and civic-minded.

According to Strauss and Howe, as the generational constellation moves forward, there is a recurring pattern of "secular crises" and "spiritual awakenings." In that pattern are four generational personalities that have recurred in the same order (with only one exception) since the 1620s.

1. The Civic Generation is always made up of outward-looking individuals who grow up with a new sense of adult protection after an awakening. As they come of age, there is a secular crisis to overcome, which unites them into a cadre of heroes and high achievers who build large institutions during midlife. As aging adults, they find themselves attacked during the next awakening.

2. The Adaptive Generation is like today's Silent Generation. They have been over-protected as children by parents who endured and overcame crisis. They come of age as cautious conformists who are concerned with "keeping the status quo." They are the indecisive mediators of the next awakening, helping all sides to be heard. As elders they are sensitive and giving.

3. The Idealist Generation is like the Boomers of today. They are individualistic and looking to have their inner needs met. They grow up as indulged youth after a crisis, and as they come of age they inspire an awakening. As adults they are narcissistic, belonging to the "me" generation. In midlife they become moralizers who seek to correct the ills of the past that their parents allowed to happen. They "emerge as visionary elders who congeal and guide the next crisis." (ibid., 30).

4. The Reactive Generation is like the 13ers today. They grow up "as underprotected and criticized youths during an awakening, come of age as alienated risk-takers, burn out young before mellowing into midlife pragmatists and family-oriented conservatives and age into caustic, but undemanding adults." (ibid., 31).

Strauss and Howe tell us that as the generations layer themselves and age in place, the mood of the constellation shifts over time. The generational cycle can give us an idea of the major changes that America can expect in the next decade and the next century. It can also predict the styles, attitudes, and behavior of each generation as it grows older.

In the late 1960s, a Boom-driven spiritual awakening challenged institutions built around old values. "Today, we have reached a typical post-awakening mood: individualism is flourishing, confidence in institutions is declining, and secular problems are deferred (ibid., 32). Frustration is mounting over a supposed loss of community, civility, and sense of national direction. The same was true of the years just before World War I. Then, as now, feminism was gaining serious political power, moralistic attacks were growing against substance abuse, and family life was seen as precious but threatened" (ibid.).

Strauss and Howe tell us that "America is now partway through its fifth generational cycle" (ibid.). If this turns out like the earlier cycles, the generations might develop in the following ways:

1. The G.I.'s will remain in their position of favor and respect earned by World War II, the institutions they built, and the progress they championed. They will continue to hold on to their public subsidizes, but with their passing, public support for federal entitlements to the elderly will gradually diminish.

2. The Silent Generation will be sympathetic to the needs of the poor and disadvantaged and work to eliminate these problems. Silents will continue to be compromisers as they work for solutions. They will lose some of their need for conformity and become more prone to taking risks. They will seek adventure that was not theirs in their youth. The Silents will want to stay connected with young people, and the extended family will enjoy renewed support. They will be discouraged by the erosion in civil rights and other types of basic kindness that they have worked hard to establish.

3. As Boomers reach their fifties, they are assuming "control of national politics with the same perfectionism and moral zeal that they are currently bringing to family and community life. As they try to reform institutions to fit their values, they will become contentious moral regulators. They will see a high purpose in what they do and what they buy. They will also annoy other generations by telling them what to do and buy" (ibid.). In their older years, Boomers will see themselves as, "wise visionaries willing to accept private austerity in return for public authority, and they will summon the nation toward unyielding principle" (ibid.).

4. The 13er Generation has so far "lived a luckless lifecycle as America's most economically disadvantaged generation. The hard luck will age with them. When bad news hits, 13er's will sink further into the alienation and pragmatism that has already attracted so much criticism. America's next generational feud—between Boomers and 13er's—is already brewing" (ibid.). After burning out young, many a 13er will retreat into and strengthen family life. History may call on them to tell righteous old Boomers to "get real" and stop arguing their way into a catastrophe.

The cycle of generations predicts that today's cute Millennial tots could become the next great cadre of civic doers and builders. They will grow up basking in adult praise and optimism. As the cycle spins into the future, many a product will be sold and election won though timely generational messages. Many a church stewardship or capital funds campaign will be affected. To succeed, such messages and campaigns will have to pay attention not to where a generation has been, but rather to where it is headed. As America moves into the new millennium the following trends will occur:

Silent Elders will respond to appeals to their other-directed pluralism, trust in expertise, emulation of the young, and unquenched thirst for adventure.

Preferred Message Style: Sensitive and personal, with an appeal to technical detail.

Preferred Giving Style: Trusting and loyal. Give from a sense of organizational responsibility and respond to direct mail and face-to-face visits.

Boom midlifers will see virtue in austerity and a well-ordered inner life. They will demand new assertion of community values over individual wants.

Preferred Message Style: Meditative and principled, with an undertone of pessimism.

Preferred Giving Style: Based on personal values and thrive on instant gratification and recognition, responding best to videos and telephone requests.

Thirteenth rising adults will need convincing proof that a product is reliable and will simplify rather than complicate their lives.

Preferred Message Style: Blunt and kinetic, with an appeal to brash survivalism.

Preferred Giving Style: Cautious and pessimistic. Give as payment for services and respond to the radio and the computer; want electronic transfer capability.

Millennial youths will believe in science and cooperation and will be easily persuaded that theirs is a good and special group that knows how to build big things together.

Preferred Message Style: Rational and constructive, with an undertone of optimism.

Preferred Giving Style: Yet unknown, but if the Generation theory continues to be valid, the style will be much like the current Silent Elders.

To make the information in this chapter have more relevance for your congregation, do the following steps.

- Create a Generation spreadsheet of the members and friends of the congregation—using numbers, not names.

- Create a Generation spreadsheet of the members of the Stewardship and Finance Committees, the session, and the Board of Deacons.

- Analyze how the stewardship program has been adjusted to allow for the needs of different generations.

MORE STEWARDSHIP TIPS: SPECIAL EVENTS

✔SPECIAL DONOR DINNER
(a soft sell)

A large congregation of 1,500 members has a fancy stewardship dinner annually at a private home. Invited to the dinner are all those persons who have given more than $4,000 to the church during the past year or the year before and those persons identified by the pastor as having the potential to increase their giving to the $4,000 level. The meal is funded by private contributions.

During the meal, the pastor gives a brief update on the mission of the church. The time becomes a sort of a pep rally for the good work of this congregation made even better because of the generosity of these members and friends. One extra benefit is that the people who already felt the significance of the congregation in their lives come to see the large number of folks who share their feelings.

As a result of this dinner, the giving continues to increase.

✔BOOMER'S DINNER
(a hard sell)

A large congregation of about 3,000 members has many affluent Boomer-generation members. This group of mostly professional people decided to host a dinner for the other people in their age range and with their same giving potential because the hosts felt that as a group they were not living up to their giving potential. The hosts for the dinner paid for this very nice meal and also organized a presentation about the mission of the church for their friends. The presentation time ended with an opportunity to ask questions and with a direct challenge for increased giving to the mission and ministry of the congregation.

Chapter 3

GIVING STYLES IN THE CHURCH

We make a living by what we get—we make a life by
what we give.

Winston Churchill

Church should be more than a place to spend an hour on Sunday. It's home. A place to be in community as you form friendships, sing in the choir, teach Sunday school, lead a youth group, share a meal, study the Bible, exchange "hellos," and sometimes bid a sad farewell. Just as our personalities have an impact on how we handle our money in our families, our money personalities impact our giving patterns and create broad general styles of giving in a Christian community, which can often be correlated to other generational demographics.

As givers, we tend to be involved in the organizations we support with our time and our money. We want simple, informative, and inspirational communications, and we demand accountability, good management, and effectiveness of the dollars given. A recent U.S. Trust Company survey of the affluent confirms that effective ministry and being able to make a difference are the prime criteria behind a gift.

The money personalities that are reflected in our giving styles are often closely related to how we worship and the love that we feel for our neighbors. Sondra Wheeler, in the book *Wealth as Peril and Obligation*, discusses the Old and New Testament themes concerning money. The emphasis in the New Testament, and consequently the church, is that wealth is a stumbling block (rich young ruler), competes for devotion (foolish farmer), and is a symptom of economic injustice associated with evil and corruption, which creates a requirement to support those in need.

Robert Wood Lynn, an independent teacher and researcher, speaking to a meeting of the development staff of the Presbyterian Church (U.S.A.) Foundation in September of 1996, identified four major giving styles.

1. *Fair Share: Giving style relates to justice.* We decide how much to give by balancing personal needs against public need. This style has no formulas or

19

benchmarks and is proportionate and regular. The difficulty is in deciding what is a fair share. This style supposes that we can honestly give a fair share.

2. *Cause giving: Giving style relates to loyalty.* We give to people or projects based on how much they touch our emotions; often impulsive or crisis-oriented, cause giving is relational. We want to give to the worthy needy that we know. The difficulties revolve around control issues and discipline and knowing who is worthy.

3. *Tithing: Giving style relates to obedience.* Scripture sets a standard to be valued and met. This is a popular but controversial style, which can burden the poor and let the wealthy off the hook and rob us of the joy of giving abundantly and sacrificially.

4. *Stewardship: Giving style relates to grace.* This holistic approach to life asks us to give of our time, talent, and treasure as they relate to our love of God and neighbor. This style brings integrity to the problem of giving, for it helps us to see giving as a part of our total obligation to love God and serve our neighbor.

Lynn emphasized that the heart of stewardship education is learning how to develop one's own vision of God's grace and its impact on every aspect of daily life. Stewardship committees, sessions, and pastors have been taught to view the administrative and financial dimensions of ministry as a source of embarrassment. For the giving level in the congregation to increase, the embarrassment and fear of talking about money must change into the concept that giving is a joyful response to God's grace.

John and Sylvia Ronsvalle believe that church leadership has failed to come to terms with the reality of affluence and that church members are underchallenged. The challenge is in helping church members move from being compulsive consumers, who are defined by what they have, to becoming stewards of the abundance entrusted to us by a generous, giving God. The objective should be not to raise money, but to transform the world.

Chapter 4

MONEY PERSONALITIES
IN THE CHURCH

Religion raises our anxieties about money and discourages
us from talking openly about them.
Robert Wuthnow, *God and Mammon in America*

An exploration of the psychology of our money is a starting place for an intentional effort to make our financial resources part of our spiritual journey. Money, the lack of it or the surplus of it, is only part of our concern about the role of money in our lives. It is how we feel about the amount of money that we have that causes us the greatest problem.

Our wealth, or our lack of it, often leads to a chronic spiritual crisis in which we experience guilt, shame, defensiveness, or pride. The idea that we are rich as measured by any existing standard creates a need to express immediate denial. If we can give to another in need, we are indeed wealthy. The spiritual crisis comes when we plan our spending and fail to help those in need. If the ancient Greeks gave to get recognition and to become immortal, and if the Romans viewed money as a matter of individual rights and used and abused it, the current Christian view of money is that God owns everything and has asked that we manage resources and recognize a responsibility for those less fortunate.

Society sends us mixed messages. We believe the love of money is the root of all evil, and yet we want more of it. According to a survey by Robert Wuthnow, 87 percent of weekly churchgoers believe greed is a sin; 79 percent say they would like more money; and 72 percent say money makes them feel good. We want the good things of life, but secretly fear that money and possessions will corrupt us. We amass more than we can use and then are fearful of giving generously and worry about how to protect what we have accumulated.

Some attitudes are generational. The G.I. Generation views frugality as a virtue and spending for fun as slightly sinful, but it gives generously. The Baby Boomers have been diligently spending next year's income today. Many of the Silent Generation quietly attempt to mediate and bring fairness to an unsympathetic world. Baby Busters, the throwaway children of divorce and poverty, fear they will never get their share.

We live in an addictive society where money and possessions are acceptable sins. We live more for the satisfaction of having, for power, influence, or control, and for the fame they give us with the "right" people. Like a person addicted to drugs or alcohol, we need more and more money and possessions to see ourselves as valuable. Frequently, these attitudes invade or block our spiritual lives, preventing a balance between family, church, community, and possessions. Having an integrated money personality where giving, getting, and spending are in balance is one of the goals of a spiritual journey.

Russ Prince and Karen File, in *The Seven Faces of Philanthropy,* deal with many motivations that tend to dominate the giving decisions that people make, which are extensions of an overall money personality. Just as one set of motivations tends to dominate how we get and invest our money, another set of motivations tends to guide how we give or fail to give. Our generous impulses can be submerged by our fears.

We have been conditioned by the past, by our families' economic histories, by advertising, and by the materialism around us. We develop money personalities that affect how we get, how we save, how we invest, and how we give. Stewardship committees need to take these attitudes into account as they develop stewardship programs.

It is easy to generalize and oversimplify when we speak of money personalities because most of us are seriously at odds with our money and often have conflicted emotions about getting and giving. We suffer from the twin evils of regret and pride. Some of our traits we have inherited from our family, and others have been caused by events in our lives or in our society. We can group our personalities and our problems into five basic categories.

1. HABITUAL ACCUMULATORS
Equate money with safety
Feel concern about the future
Feel poor but have money
Are risk-adverse investors
Plan to give later when they have more
Giving style—Do their fair share
Need—Vision

2. HABITUAL SPENDERS
Equate stuff with safety
Spend to feel good
Charge more than they can afford
Have nothing to invest
Have little to give
Giving style—Give out of fear
Need—Encouragement

3. HABITUAL PROCRASTINATORS
Won't make plans
Don't keep records
Hope that things will work out

Fail to pledge or are late with pledges
Giving style—Give on impulse
Need—Opportunities

4. HABITUAL WORRIERS

Shun any form of risk
Are obsessed with money
Fear poverty
Fail to enjoy today
Giving style—Give grudgingly through duty
Need—Assurances

5. HABITUAL GAMBLERS

Have no savings
Need excitement
Winning boosts self-esteem
Believe in luck
Giving style—Pledge, but fail to give or give impulsively
Need—Projects with pizzazz

Some people give because they believe that it is God's will. They give out of a sense of gratitude—because of God's grace. Others give because they believe that it is the logical, practical thing to do, or by extension, that it is good business. There are those who give because it is family tradition, or because it makes them feel good, or simply for the social interaction and good times provided by the process.

Our net worth can affect how we view making a bequest. Accumulated resources become especially significant as a church enters into a wills program with a life-income component. Wealthy people like customized opportunities, and middle-income people like to have choices. Various stewardship activities need to take into consideration a donor's need for knowledge, the financial situation of members, and the need to use judgment, intentionality, experience, and creativity in reaching people.

We must deal with the myths that leaving a legacy of faith is only for the rich and that if we leave such a bequest we are hurting our families. It is the widow's mite that speaks most clearly—her legacy is eloquent.

What must follow this understanding of personality is how it affects the ability of a stewardship program in the church. If we assume that blocks of each of the generational personality types exist in our congregations, how do we proceed to create opportunities that nurture and expand our willingness to give? Clergy and lay committee members need to educate themselves and to create an environment where giving is part of the larger vision of mission and ministry.

The Money Attitudes Inventory, Tool #7, in the Toolbox section of this book, can begin the process of getting the members of a church in touch with their attitudes about money and giving and can begin the process of integrating our money with our spiritual journey.

This process requires that the following elements to a vital year-round stewardship program become part of stewardship planning.

Define a vision of Christian stewardship.

Create an excitement for mission and ministry.

Build relationships and increased involvement.

Create different ways and causes for giving.

Provide opportunities to learn and share about money and giving.

Identify appropriate giving strategies for annual and capital campaigns.

Increase awareness of ways to give.

Create a wills/bequests program based on the wholeness of Christian stewardship.

Implement a program for awareness of life-income plans.

Promote the program through newsletter articles, minutes for mission, seminars.

Empower members to see their gifts of time, talent, and treasure as significant and valued.

Create ways to show appreciation for gifts.

Evaluate the process and programs.

Questions to focus our efforts:

1. Do members have a vision for the mission and ministry of the church on the local, presbytery, synod, and national levels?

2. Do pastors, staff, and committee members create attractive opportunities to grow commitment and involvement?

3. Does the program include visioning, theological implications, and practical learning about money matters?

4. Are relationships encouraged?

To make the information in this chapter have more relevance for your congregation, individually and then as a committee, complete Tool #7, Money Attitudes Inventory.

Chapter 5

ANNUAL GIVING

*Having first gained all you can, and secondly, saved all
you can, then give all you can.*

John Wesley

When stewardship is mentioned in the congregation, what most often comes to mind is the "Annual Campaign." Traditionally, this campaign has been thought of as "raising the budget." A better way to think of this process is as a plan to permit the congregation to be in mission and ministry with members, friends, and the community. The pastor and key lay leaders must function as a team in this endeavor. Leadership must be shared. It is not exclusively the responsibility of either lay or clergy.

This chapter looks at three areas:

1. Ways you tell the church story to increase financial giving

2. How you organize to increase financial giving

3. Whom you ask to increase financial giving

WAYS YOU TELL THE CHURCH STORY
TO INCREASE FINANCIAL GIVING

The way the church story is told to increase financial giving is influenced by many factors, including the generational differences mentioned in Chapter Two.

Some people think the annual giving campaign is to "see how much money we need" and to raise that amount. Determining need is an important part of this process, but the way we arrive at the budget and the way we explain the budget to the congregation are extremely important aspects of the annual giving plan.

Kennon Callahan, in his book *Giving and Stewartship in an Effective Church*, says within each person are five motivations for giving—challenge, commitment, reasonability, community, and compassion. Church leaders and people newer to the church respond to different motives. Callahan believes that church leaders respond to the words "commitment" and "challenge" when talking about money and budget. Those persons who are newer to the church and to the Christian faith respond more to the words "community" and "compassion." People working to "tell the story" are always the leaders in a congregation and must make an effort to "tell the story" in words that can be heard by the newer, developing stewards. These new stewards are most often choosing to give to the church among many other opportunities they have in their lives.

There are basically three ways to develop and interpret the church budget:

1. Committee Structure of the Session Budget

2. "What Was Spent Last Year" Budget

3. Congregational Mission Goals Budget

COMMITTEE STRUCTURE OF THE SESSION BUDGET

This budget is developed when committee members sit down together and are encouraged to develop either a "dream budget" or "a realistic budget." Normally, this budget is written by committee line items, and the chairs of each committee gather for "the budget discussion." This discussion can occur before the budget is presented to the congregation or after it is presented. Whenever it occurs, the discussion often degenerates into a territorial harangue as dollars are cut away based on the actual pledges in hand or expected pledges.

The Dream Budget

In developing the dream budget, committee members are encouraged to think beyond the here and now. They are encouraged to take a risk for the future mission and ministry of the congregation. The "dream budget" is presented to the congregation as a first step in the annual giving campaign in an attempt to raise the giving level to the "dream."

The Up Side	The Down Side
Budget is clearer	Committee with most money is often viewed as more important
Budget is thought of in segments of "church work"	People don't think about mission and ministry in a holistic way
Budget discussion can be focused	Budget discussion often causes dissension
Budget is normally more geared to "committed members"	Budget makes it more difficult to inspire developing stewards
Budget encourages people to think of new plans	Fat is often built into the budget and programs

The Realistic Budget

In developing the realistic budget, committee members are encouraged to limit their budget request to "the way we've always done it" or "how much does it cost to maintain the buildings, the staff, our programs, and mission?" The order of the priorities oftens discourages increased giving. The "realistic budget" or "what was given last year" is presented to the congregation as a first step in the annual giving campaign in an attempt to raise the giving level to exceed the bare necessities.

The Up Side	**The Down Side**
Budget is clearer	Committee with most money is often viewed as more important
Budget is thought of in segments of "church work"	People don't think about mission and ministry in a holistic way
Budget discussion can be focused	Budget discussion often causes dissension
Budget is normally more geared to "committed members"	Budget makes it more difficult to inspire developing stewards
	Planning is limited to the status quo

"WHAT WAS SPENT LAST YEAR" BUDGET

This budget is normally developed by the Budget/Finance Committee as it considers what various committees spent last year. This is presented to the governing body of the congregation. The same type of heated "budget discussion" often follows.

The Up Side	**The Down Side**
Budget is developed quickly	Encourages last minute, sometimes unnecessary spending
Budget makes bookkeeping easier	Promotes the "status quo"
	Makes it difficult for new programs or ideas to be developed
	Focuses on expenses
	Makes it difficult to attract young givers
	Narrows ownership of budget decisions

CONGREGATIONAL MISSION GOALS BUDGET

Understanding the major mission priorities of a congregation and building the budget on those priorities is a new way of thinking proposed by Kennon Callahan in *Effective Church Finances*. This budget is based on the established mission goals, which are evaluated each year. Budgets based on congregational mission goals can be formatted in the traditional style or as a narrative budget. An example would be a congregation that has as a mission goal "to develop and operate a not-for-profit child care center with 20 percent of the children on scholarships and a weekly support group for parents of the children."

The budgets of the Christian education ministry, mission ministry, and committee concerned with facilities will be affected in this process. A mission-based budget helps build bridges between persons of varying interests. More congregational ownership is created when people realize it isn't just the work of one committee or one group creating the budget.

The best way to tell the mission story is in a narrative budget that describes the way lives are affected by the mission goal. It is also possible to discuss the cost of *not* doing the mission to those who are uncertain about the expenses. Ask people, "What will be the cost to the lives of children if we don't develop this mission?"

Ultimately, the budget must be finalized in a line-item format; however, most of the congregation has no interest in this document. A detailed budget should be available for those who request it. Most people in a congregation, especially developing stewards, are interested in knowing what difference their giving makes in people's lives.

The Up Side	**The Down Side**
People have more ownership	Initially harder to get old-time leaders to agree to this approach
Budget presents a clearer picture of its impact on people's lives	Requires extensive planning and coordination
Budget develops thoughtful mission	
Budget makes a more direct connection between money and mission goals	

The goal of this book is to move your congregation from the stifling, boring, and deadening "committee-based" or "spent last year" budget, to the joyous, open, exciting "mission-centered" budget. Financial giving will increase, and overall ownership and enthusiasm for the church will deepen.

HOW YOU ORGANIZE TO
INCREASE FINANCIAL GIVING

Step One: Create a Stewardship Committee, separate from the Finance Committee. Having these two committees in place provides for a division of labor and good use of the gifts of individuals.

- The Finance Committee is made up of those people who monitor the day-to-day, month-to-month financial concerns of a congregation. The Finance Committee would also oversee the investments of any reserves or endowments in memorial funds.

- The Stewardship Committee concentrates its efforts on the planning, promotion, and execution of a coordinated continuing emphasis in a year-long stewardship awareness intended to increase the giving level of members and friends of a congregation. Part of this committee's work is the annual giving program.

Invite people who are passionate about the mission goals of a congregation to join with the pastor and other key leaders to help plan the annual giving program. Strive to have a balance of older and younger people; a mixture of newer members and long-time members; people with the ability to communicate verbally and in written form; and people with knowledge and passion for the church's mission goals. A committee of seven to ten persons is ideal so that no one person is overworked and a variety of gifts and talents can be represented among the members.

Step Two: Develop awareness within the Stewardship Committee of the mission goals. People cannot interpret what they don't understand and what they do not own. Therefore, the first meeting of the committee must allow time for members to discuss the significance of the mission goals of the congregation. People who are passionate about these mission goals should be invited to talk with the committee about the many ways the lives of people are affected by the investment the church makes in this mission. Understanding these goals leads to the next step.

Step Three: Design a way to interpret the mission of the congregation to the friends and members of the congregation. Interpreting the mission of the congregation is more than simply developing a time line. A strategy for telling the story of the mission of the congregation in terms of the lives that have been affected by that mission must be designed. Tell stories that highlight the various ways the hurts and hopes of the community have been addressed through the work of the congregation. People do not give to budgets. They do give to make a difference in the lives of people. They do give to meaningful mission goals.

The mission goals can be interpreted in the following ways:

- Narrative budget brochure
- Minutes for mission
- Church dinners with a program
- Personal one-on-one visits
- Cluster group meetings
- Creative use of bulletin boards
    More pictures than words
    More concentration on the lives of people than on the budget

Denominational annual thematic emphasis materials and other stewardship resources are available from the General Assembly Office in Louisville. These excellent resources can be effectively integrated in the telling of the congregation's mission story. Specific resources are identified in the Toolbox and the Stewardship Resources of this book.

Ordinarily, it takes two to three months to do a thorough job of interpreting the mission and ministry of a congregation. Therefore, to set a starting date, count backward from the date when the results of your annual giving campaign must be known.

As you plan ways to interpret the congregation's mission giving, use Tool #1, Giving in Your Congregation in the Toolbox section of this book to help you see where money has gone in years past and to help you develop a plan for years to come. Tool #4, Mission-Based Narrative Budget Worksheet, will be helpful to your committee.

Step Four: Design a process for the actual annual giving campaign. There are at least four basic strategies for the annual giving campaign. First is mailing out letters and asking for commitments by return mail. Second is one Sunday of commitment that follows several weeks of preaching and written communication. Third is a variation of the "pass the packet" plan. Fourth is one-on-one home visits by church leaders. Each strategy has its own level of complexity and different time when it is appropriate in the congregation's life.

The Stewardship Manual (pp. 26–29) of the Presbyterian Church (U.S.A.) describes these in more detail. Pros and cons for each method are included. *The Stewardship Manual* can be ordered from Louisville or may be available immediately from your presbytery resource center. After careful planning, select the method best for your congregation and begin the planning to coordinate the mission story with the campaign.

Step Five: Plan a way to express appreciation to the givers. Saying thanks is not only a good idea but a critical element of any stewardship program. In an earlier time, when people gave from obligation and duty motives, thanks were not needed and were rarely expressed. In this modern time, when people choose to give to the church from among a number of causes, it is important to affirm their gifts and to continue to make givers aware of the impact of their gifts. Differences in points of view about the need for appreciation will make conversation in the Stewardship Committee necessary. Remember a church leader who responds from the motive of "commitment" often feels thanks are unnecessary. The stewards were just doing their duty. Newer stewards, giving from motives of "compassion" and "community," want thanks and assurance that their giving matters.

Some ways of saying thanks are:

- Send out thank-you letters from the Stewardship Committee.

- Include a celebration before, during, or after worship.

- Stamp a simple "Thank-you" on each check written to the church and returned in members' bank statements.

- During the year, include a story in the church newsletter about the life of a person affected by the mission of the church.

- Add a thank-you to the back of the church letterhead or quarterly report. This thank-you can contain a real example of someone helped by the mission of the church and tell who did the helping, if possible.

Step Six: Plan a time to evaluate the entire process. Often ignored, timely evaluation is crucial. Evaluation needs to be completed before the details slip away. Sit down at the next meeting of the Stewardship Committee and honestly discuss the "celebrations" and the "could be improved" of the annual giving campaign.

Write down your suggestions and observations and be certain they are communicated to the planning team for next year.

WHOM YOU ASK TO INCREASE FINANCIAL GIVING

Too often only active members respond to the Annual Giving opportunity. For financial giving to increase, a more broad-based plan needs to be adopted.

1. *Contact members who pledged last year.* Naturally, the members of a congregation are expected to provide the majority of the funding for a congregation's mission and ministry. As you plan your strategy, Tool #2, Giving in Your Congregation by Giving Units, in The Toolbox, will be helpful. This tool encourages you to look at the giving of your congregation by units.

2. *Ask members who did **not** pledge last year.* Another important group of people are the members who gave in previous years, but did not pledge last year. These people need a different, more personal, approach by the committee. Anticipate the questions and comments that will come related to other aspects of the life of the congregation. Be prepared to discuss negative or challenging comments about the direction of the church or personal situations.

3. *Approach friends of the congregation.* Be certain that more than members are made aware of the opportunity to be a part of the mission of the congregation through their financial participation. Friends of a congregation are often more than willing to join the effort. Friends of a congregation include:
   - Persons who come occasionally to worship and other events at the church
   - Former members who have maintained connection through the newsletter
   - Friends of members who give memorial gifts
   - People in the community who have a particular passion for a mission

4. *Invite people who have benefited from the church's mission.* Out of gratitude, these people may welcome a chance to give something back to God.

UNDERSTANDING YOUR
CONGREGATION'S ATTITUDE ABOUT MONEY

Your congregation's attitude about money and giving is extremely important. There are many aspects of understanding the attitude of an individual toward money and giving. The attitudes of individuals come from their experiences in their families, their occupations, and other congregations where they have been members. The attitude of a congregation, both spoken and unspoken, is determined by the attitudes of individual members combined with the prevailing "we've always done it this way before" response. This makes the integration of new ideas and subsequent change difficult.

Using Tool #3, Congregational Attitudes toward Money and Giving, will help you understand these attitudes and help you plan a focus for your congregation's stewardship education.

The most discussed and controversial aspect of money and giving is who should know the level of giving of members. There is a growing trend toward openness as opposed to the intense secrecy approach of the past.

Some steps toward openness are:

- Encourage your pastor and key leaders to be open about their giving level. In most congregations, the pastor is among the top five givers in the congregation. People are aware of the salary of the pastor, so openness about his or her personal giving makes a strong statement to members and friends about increasing giving. In many congregations, key lay leaders are among the top givers. As a team, clergy and lay leaders can create an atmosphere of humble, gracious openness about giving.

- Give the members of the Stewardship Committee knowledge about giving levels in the congregation.

- Rotate people in and out of the Stewardship Committee frequently.

- Use the step-up charts found in *The Stewardship Manual* as a way to help persons plan incremental increases in their giving.

- Publish in your newsletter Tool #2 from the back of this book. By indicating the number of units giving specific amounts, people are able to compare for themselves. Often people feel they are giving a great deal because they are unaware of what is really the norm.

All these steps are designed to challenge people to increase their level of giving. People will respond to a clearly defined mission of the church by giving more of their money when they are made aware of needs and expectations related to that mission.

QUESTIONS FOR THOUGHT AND DISCUSSION

1. What are the strengths of your current annual giving programs?

2. What information in the previous chapters could be incorporated in your annual giving program to build on the strengths above?

STEWARDSHIP TIP

✔ In planning the agenda for the meeting of the congregation's governing body, always have the Treasurer's Report presented at the end of the meeting. There has never been a congregation with more money than it needed, so talking about money first only stifles any creative talk about new areas of mission or new ways to advance existing mission causes.

✔ Consistently use the devotional time to help leaders focus on God's gifts given freely to each person.

✔ Use scripture in the call for the offering each Sunday. Tool #8 gives a list of appropriate verses.

✔ Encourage the study and adoption of the *Covenants of Stewardship* materials available from the Presbyterian Church (U.S.A.).

✔ Using "Stu Bear" resources for children and "Choices" for youth, develop a plan to teach these young stewards about giving.

Chapter 6

SPECIAL OFFERINGS AND APPEALS

My deeds must be my life.
Stephen Girard

People seem willing to give to an endless number of special appeals for money. When a congregation chooses to offer many opportunities for giving, people learn about a wide variety of mission opportunities, some of which tap into their individual interests. Some worry about having too many special offerings. Everyone is not expected to give to every special offering, but the more opportunities offered the greater likelihood there is of involving more people. When the need is articulated clearly and there is confidence that the money will be used in concrete ways that offer help and hope, people are very generous.

A special offering should be presented to the congregation in creative ways that indicate how the lives of people will be changed because of the gift. There is no set amount of time needed to promote a special offering. A six-month plan works well for regularly received offerings, but emergencies will arise and a special appeal can be organized quickly.

Interpretation of the special offering can take place in a variety of ways:

• Printed materials containing pictures and stories of people

• Minutes for mission during a morning worship service

• Church dinners combined with a program about the recipients

• Displays throughout the church facilities

• Letters mailed to the congregation telling of the offering

In the Presbyterian Church (U.S.A.), there are four special offerings recognized as extremely important to the mission of the church, which have significance beyond regular mission giving. It should be understood that these are "authorized" special offerings, but the session of each congregation must decide which offerings to receive.

ONE GREAT HOUR OF SHARING OFFERING

One Great Hour of Sharing is an ecumenical offering begun in 1949 by nine denominations to offer an opportunity to share God's love with a world in need. Its roots were in the radio-broadcasts introduced immediately after World War II to secure funds to assist in the rebuilding of Europe. "Recognizing that the hope we have in Christ is lived out in our love for one another, we respond with gifts that help our brothers and sisters around the world find hope for a better future" ("The Four Churchwide Offerings of the Presbyterian Church [U.S.A.]").

The gifts of Presbyterians across the country enable Presbyterian Disaster Assistance, the Presbyterian Committee on Self-Development of People, and the Presbyterian Hunger Program to respond to people's immediate and long-term needs. These monies are used for response to disasters, to help in refugee resettlement, and to aid in community development across the United States and around the world.

The Presbyterian Disaster Assistance receives 36 percent of the undesignated portion of One Great Hour of Sharing, and Self-Development of People and the Presbyterian Hunger Program each receive 32 percent.

Most congregations receive this offering on Palm Sunday or Easter Sunday. Some congregations have chosen to receive the One Great Hour of Sharing Offering throughout the Lenten season.

PENTECOST OFFERING

"At the heart of the Christian mission rests the evangelion, the good news that Jesus Christ has come to bring life and hope to a world in need. Presbyterians seek to proclaim this timeless message in word and deed" ("Four Churchwide Offerings"). One way the Presbyterian Church (U.S.A.) reaches out is through this offering, which goes to assist children at risk, youths, and young adults.

The Pentecost Offering is received by most congregations on Pentecost Sunday. The offering is divided among General Assembly, presbytery, and local congregations, which allows for great diversity and creativity in the many national, regional, and local ways by which hope and help can be delivered.

The General Assembly receives 70 percent of the offering, and that amount is divided among the projects of the three ministry areas: Worldwide, National, and Congregational Ministries. Of the General Assembly portion, part goes to assist children at risk, and another portion goes for Youth and Young Adult Ministries. The presbytery and local congregation retain 30 percent of the offering.

"The Pentecost Offering represents a call to mission with children at risk and a celebration of ministry with youth and young adults, sending them forth to share and proclaim the gospel to all the world" ("Four Churchwide Offerings").

PEACEMAKING OFFERING

Brokenness is all around us in the world. But as Christians, we know this brokenness is not the way God intended things to be. We believe that God is constantly at work in the world granting wholeness and peace. As Christians, we are called to be agents of that wholeness and peace; therefore, we are called to be agents of reconciliation in families, in the lives of individuals, and in our communities. This call extends to the international arena and to the whole of God's creation. "The Peacemaking Offering supports the peacemaking efforts of the church at every level and provides an opportunity to witness to God's peacegiving in the world" ("Four Churchwide Offerings").

Congregations that receive the Peacemaking Offering are encouraged to keep 25 percent of the gifts for their own peacemaking work. Presbyteries and synod peacemaking efforts receive 25 percent, and 50 percent is forwarded to the Presbyterian Peacemaking Program of the General Assembly.

The Peacemaking Offering is ordinarily received by congregations on World Communion Sunday, the first Sunday in October.

CHRISTMAS JOY OFFERING

"Bringing joy to persons both young and old through a Christmas offering has been a Presbyterian tradition for more than sixty years. As we celebrate the unity of God's family through Jesus Christ, we remember and recognize persons in our community of faith in a tangible way" ("Four Churchwide Offerings").

This offering makes a difference in the lives of church servants and students at racial ethnic schools. The Board of Pensions offers help to those persons currently serving in the church and to those persons who have served faithfully and are now retired and find themselves in need. Providing an opportunity that might not be available otherwise, the Presbyterian racial ethnic schools and colleges provide minority students an opportunity to learn, grow, and develop their gifts.

The Christmas Joy Offering is divided equally between the Board of Pensions and the racial ethnic institutions of learning. The offering is ordinarily received the Sunday before Christmas.

HOW TO PROMOTE THESE OFFERINGS

Packets of materials are received by congregations approximately six months before each offering is to be received. These packets contain samples of envelopes, posters, bulletin inserts, Bible studies, and other materials useful in telling your congregation about the recipients of the offering. Most of the materials are available free to congregations or individuals by calling 1-800-524-2612.

Create a committee of persons who are especially passionate about each offering cause. The committee can develop a plan for promotion.

HOW TO ENCOURAGE RECEIVING THESE OFFERINGS

Gather the promotional information, and ask your session for permission to make a presentation that includes a request to receive the offering. The interpretation of these offerings by knowledgeable people to your congregation acquaints your members with the broad scope of the mission of the Presbyterian Church. People will be more aware that together we do more in mission than one congregation is able to do alone. If the overarching vision of a congregation is clearly defined, more than likely each of these special offerings can be connected to that vision.

More information that will help you interest the session in a particular offering can be obtained by writing Mission Interpretation and Promotion, 100 Witherspoon Street, Louisville, KY 40202-1396, or by calling 502-569-5183.

QUESTIONS FOR THOUGHT AND DISCUSSION

1. What are the strengths of your current special offering programs?

2. What information in the previous chapters could be incorporated in your special offering program to build on the strengths above?

Chapter 7

CAPITAL CAMPAIGNS

Thrift is a wonderful virtue especially in an ancestor.
Mark Twain

The decision to have a capital campaign begins with congregations having a specific problem or need. It might be deferred maintenance, growth that creates a need for new space, new missions, need for renewal, or the desire to fund an endowment. All too often, there is a tendency to rush from the recognition of a problem or a combination of problems to making a list and asking for gifts.

The critical step that is often forgotten is to step back and to define prayerfully the congregation's vision. A capital campaign is an opportunity to think about mission and to think about it in a big way. This is the time to ask the question: "What is our mission?"

The spectrum of giving begins with the annual gift that is given from cash flow. Giving is expanded during a capital campaign to gifts from accumulated assets. Because capital gifts are larger gifts, the need to develop a plan of cultivating and nurturing members is essential. Communication and accountability are critical for donor trust to be built. The result can be a revitalized church.

STEPS TO A SUCCESSFUL CAMPAIGN

Step One: Set up a focus group. A natural first step is a congregational town meeting that allows everyone the opportunity to express his or her vision for the future ministries of the church, to set goals, and to develop consensus. This should result in a compelling vision that logically calls for a capital campaign so that the mission and ministry of the local body can be accomplished. One critical element is that there be something for everyone: young, old, mission, building, endowment.

The mission component of a capital campaign allows the corporate body to be a model of good stewardship. The giving of funds outside the local body adds excitement and interest for something greater than the church's actual pressing need. Consultation with the presbytery and the inclusion of a presbytery cause such as new church development can increase commitment to the broader mission of Christ.

An endowment component, which could be for the future maintenance of the facility as well as for mission and program, will appeal to many. The reality of our demographics suggests that unless we take seriously the need for a flow of stable funding, the future viability of our churches could be in trouble.

The exciting challenge in managing a capital campaign is to see that giving to the annual programs and missions of the church is not curtailed. The goal is not to raise dollars, but to raise the commitment level, and the money will follow. The emphasis should be on how this project will touch lives—the individual and the broader world.

Step Two: Perform a readiness assessment. This step cannot be overlooked and is important even if the levels of excitement and commitment to the project are high. Taking the time to test to ascertain how the project will be financed and that the commitments that are needed are present is worth the time and energy that it takes to complete the assessment. The assessment assists in describing the proposed plan so that all alternatives are considered. An excellent resource within the Presbyterian Church (U.S.A.) is the *Church Financial Campaign Service Handbook,* which has been helping congregations implement successful capital campaigns for more than fifty years.

Step Three: Create a committee structure. The third step is the creation of the infrastructure that runs the campaign. The capital campaign should not be added to the responsibility of the existing Finance, Budget, or Annual Campaign Committees. A separate Capital Campaign Committee should be formed and consist of:

- An overall chairperson
- The pastor
- Coordinators for advance gifts and visiting stewards
- Hospitality chair
- Promotion chair
- Support chair
- Finance chair
- Follow-up and fulfillment chair

Each of these people then recruits the workers for the campaign in their respective areas. This structure allows for greater involvement and ownership of the project. Leaders of the campaign must have a willingness to give generously, which sets a standard for the other donors. Additionally, leaders should enthusiastically endorse the project and also have the respect of the congregation.

Step Four: Seek advance/major gifts. The fourth step is the major gifts component. These gifts determine the success or failure of a capital funds campaign. As a rule of thumb, approximately 20 pecent of donors provide 80 percent of the funding. Advanced gifts need to be secured before going to the congregation for the general campaign. This step encompasses deciding whom to ask, how much to ask for, and who will do the asking and making a personal visit to ask for the lead gifts.

The visiting stewards must be prepared to answer any questions about the plans and to help the prospect agree to the program's validity and then to suggest an amount that the individual or family might prayerfully consider. The stewards should not leave the pledge card, but should ask to return, and should never hurry the process.

Even though the campaign needs gifts, it is important to remember that it is the mission of the church of Jesus Christ that is being discussed. Prayer, optimism, and expectancy are important elements of a successful major gift program. Although not a separate step, the inclusion of a life-income plan program allows many to give more and others to begin to give. The Presbyterian Church (U.S.A.) Foundation's development officers can provide this service to the campaign at no charge.

Step Five: Line up campaign events. The fifth step is the actual campaign events. This is an intentional process with a deliberate strategy. A chart of all the activities for each committee on a time line forms the basis for the campaign. The leaders need to project a high level of awareness, generosity, and commitment and have the ability to coordinate people and tasks. Many campaigns culminate with a congregational dinner that celebrates the mission and ministry of the church and the impending success of the project.

Step Six: Acknowledge gifts received and follow up on unfulfilled pledges. Acknowledging gifts, saying thank you, and following up on the fulfillment of pledges require attention and must not be overlooked in the euphoria of success. Thank-you letters and personal notes from visiting stewards are necessary immediately following the receipt of pledge cards. Other types of recognition, such as "victory" dinners, certificates, plaques, and/or named gift opportunities, might also be appropriate ways of saying thank you.

To encourage fulfillment of the pledge:

- Send quarterly reminders with thank you's
- Publish a status box indicating the progress of the campaign in the newsletter
- Include articles on the status of the project in the newsletter
- Update the progress of the campaign using Minutes for Mission

QUESTIONS FOR THOUGHT AND DISCUSSION

1. What are the strengths of your most recent capital campaign?

2. What are the strengths of your church that will have a positive effect on your proposed capital campaign?

3. What information in the previous chapters could be incorporated in your capital campaign to build on the strengths above?

Chapter 8

PLANNED GIVING

When I am dead, my actions must speak for me.
Stephen Girard

No gifts are accidental—all gifts are planned. When it comes to making charitable gifts, each of us needs to plan. Sometimes we decide to have no plan and simply give our pocket change on a Sunday morning, or we make a plan for a year and break it into weekly pieces. However, when we speak of planned gifts, we are referring to those gifts that are formalized in a will, living trust, life-income plan, or life estate with the actual release of funds to come sometime in the future. Except for a bequest, this type of gift generally carries with it immediately favorable tax benefits for the donor. Planned gifts have become a major source of funds for capital campaigns and endowments for many churches and church-related institutions.

PLANNED GIVING—NOT JUST FOR THE WEALTHY

Unfortunately, two stewardship myths are that stewardship refers only to the annual giving campaign for the budgetary needs of the church and that planned giving is only for people who have amassed large financial resources. In truth, the stewardship plan for each congregation should offer opportunities for all individuals to respond to annual giving campaigns and also to plan for gifts beyond their lifetime.

Planned giving differs from the annual stewardship campaign because it is long term in contrast to the annual budget needs. Consequently, planned giving is best accomplished in an intentional, consistent manner rather than as a campaign. Gifts received through life-income plans and bequests also tend to be larger than annual pledges and contributions to the general operation of the church. Because this type of stewardship is identified with lifetime accumulations rather than with weekly or monthly income, complex federal and state laws that require explanation apply to these gifts.

The development of long-term giving requires not only extraordinary patience and understanding, but an appreciation of the differing values we hold about money as well as an appreciation for members' strongly held convictions and beliefs.

Because planned giving is a method of allowing the member to obtain benefits other than those normally envisioned by church members, an educational program is essential. With planned gifts, the donor may benefit from current income or deferred retirement income, avoid capital gains taxes, and reduce or eliminate income and estate taxes. Such gifts can be completed through a will or a living trust, a life insurance policy, or a charitable trust. Gifts can be funded with cash, securities, real estate, or any other property that has a real value and that can be sold.

The spectrum of giving moves from annual pledges to special/capital gifts to lifetime gifts. One might think of this spectrum as encompassing recurring (frequent) and nonrecurring giving (infrequent).

The Christian stewardship of accumulated resources should be part of a year-round program that is integrated with the annual campaign and with any capital funds campaign. Such a program needs to emphasize both a wills and bequests program and life-income plan opportunities for individuals. Because we are called to accountability not only for our annual gifts from our income but for our accumulated resources as well, congregations need to be offered opportunities for timeless stewardship.

CONSIDERATIONS FOR DEVELOPING A PROGRAM

As we begin to establish a program, we need to understand God's regard for humanity and our role as stewards of God's bounty. Three elements should be present before we begin.

1. Prayer—God gave us this gift of communion to ensure a successful program. (Philippians 4:6)

2. Persistence—Each person would like to leave his or her permanent footprints. (2 Corinthians 4:1)

3. Patience—We may not see the results of a planned giving program for a number of years. (1 Corinthians 3:6)

DEVELOPING A WILLS AND PLANNED GIFTS PROGRAM

Step One: Get the approval of the session. Examples of resolutions are available through the Presbyterian Church (U.S.A.) Foundation development officers.

Step Two: Appoint a committee. Include people who have a flair for marketing as well as people who have a gift with finances. The session should appoint a Wills and Planned Gifts Committee of three to five persons, at least one of whom should be a member of the session. The primary purpose of the committee is to create and implement an integrated, intentional, year-round educational program.

Step Three: Create an advisory group. Members with expertise in the church's mission and those with special knowledge or experience in the legal and technical aspects of wills and life income plans should assist in the development of gifts.

Step Four: Develop a program that promotes this area of stewardship monthly. Many informational pieces will be done in conjunction with the annual campaign and/or capital campaign. A planning calendar is available through the Presbyterian Church (U.S.A.) Foundation.

Step Five: Promote the importance of charitable estate planning for everybody. This can be done by arranging to have two or three major events each year, such as a program on money management, an estate-planning seminar, a wills or planned giving program, wills emphasis Sunday, small groups, and minutes for mission, to name just a few.

Step Six: Create a donor recognition program.

CHARACTERISTICS OF A SUCCESSFUL PLANNED GIFTS PROGRAM

1. Supportive pastor

2. Active, planned giving committee with regular monthly meetings

3. Budget for programs and materials

4. Creative information program

5. Regular intentional interpretative materials

6. Thoughtful endowment policies

7. Committed session

INTENTIONAL PROMOTION OF A PLANNED GIVING PROGRAM

1. Create a brochure that initially may be a bulletin insert. Distribute the general brochure by placing on literature tables and in pew racks or deliver during the annual campaign. Always include in new member materials.

2. Observe Wills/Endowment Sunday. The observance might include posters, bulletin inserts, newsletters, minutes for stewardship, adult education programs, or related sermons.

3. Conduct special workshops on topics such as wills and trusts, charitable estate planning, and financial management.

4. Have regular articles on related topics in the newsletter or bulletin, which tell stories and provide information. Prepare two- to three-sentence paragraphs that can be plugged in bulletins.

5. Have the Presbyterian Church (U.S.A.) Foundation publications, *The Cornerstone* and *Insights*, mailed to church leaders.

6. Visit www.fdn.pcusa.org regularly for new ideas.

7. Do it all again. Patience is a requirement.

ESTATE PLANNING

Estate planning is the process of getting what we want to whom we want, when we want, and how we want, while saving as many fees and taxes as possible. The documents used in estate planning include wills, revocable living trusts, durable powers of attorney, living wills, health care surrogates, and charitable trusts. The goal is to give more to those we love, which includes our extended family—the church. Family, charity, and government can share in our estates. Without appropriate understanding and action, the government often gets more than its fair share. The goal is to move from involuntary to voluntary philanthropy.

Estate planning helps us to manage our affairs, to plan for an incapacity, to enjoy the benefits of making gifts today, while we arrange for the orderly and efficient distribution of our estates to our heirs. Our greatest legacy to our heirs is the thoughtful transfer of our property, which includes the mission of Jesus Christ. It is a civic responsibility that the state takes if we ignore our estate planning responsibilities. For the Christian, it is also a joyous privilege where we honor and glorify God for the blessings bestowed on us. Estate planning allows us to protect from the erosion of income, capital gains, and estate taxes the assets God has entrusted to us.

LIFE-INCOME PLANS

Life-income plans are the result of the federal government's policy of encouraging private philanthropy. Long-range planning for the mission of our churches requires that we incorporate this area of stewardship awareness into our other stewardship activities.

Donors can receive multiple benefits when they execute an irrevocable planned gift:

- Increased income
- Reduction of income taxes
- Reduction or elimination of capital gains taxes
- Reduction or elimination of estate taxes
- Opportunity to make a larger gift than could be made with an outright gift
- Low-cost professional management
- Opportunity to establish a permanent memorial fund

All types of assets can be used to make a gift through a bequest or a life-income plan:

- Cash
- Publicly traded securities
- Real estate
- Personal property
- Life insurance

- Closely held securities
- Income in Respect of a Descendent assets (IRAs, annuities, 403bs, 401ks, series EE bonds)

The inclusion of life-income plans allows for our deepest wishes to be realized. Life-income plans may be done as a single element of an estate or financial plan or in combinations that allow for the greatest benefit for the donor, the family, and the mission of Christ.

TYPES OF LIFE-INCOME PLANS

- *Charitable Remainder Annuity Trust*: An irrevocable trust whereby the Presbyterian Church (U.S.A.) Foundation serving as trustee pays one or more individual beneficiaries a fixed amount, at least annually, which is not less than 5 percent of the initial net fair market value of all property placed in the trust. When the trust terminates, the remaining principal becomes available for the mission of the church as designated by the donor.

- *Charitable Gift Annuity*: An irrevocable gift contract that provides a fixed annual annuity for the lifetimes of one or two individuals based in part on the annuitant's age when the gift is made. Following the lifetimes of the annuitant(s), the charitable remainder interest in the gift remains for the church's work. A charitable gift annuity may be immediate (annuity payments begin within one year of the gift date) or deferred (annuity payments begin more than one year after the gift date).

- *Charitable Remainder Unitrust*: An irrevocable trust whereby the Presbyterian Church (U.S.A.) Foundation as trustee pays to one or more individual beneficiaries, at least annually, a fixed percentage, at least 5 percent of the net fair market value of the trust's assets as revalued annually. When the trust terminates, the remaining principal becomes available to provide funds for the fulfillment of the great commission.

- *Pooled Income Fund*: Irrevocable gifts that are invested in a mutual fund under professional management. A donor retains a life-income interest in the property transferred for one or more beneficiaries. Following the life of the last income beneficiary, the value of the pooled fund account is separated from the fund and used to establish an endowment or distributed in full to an organization that is part of the Presbyterian Church (U.S.A.).

BEQUESTS

A bequest in a will or other estate plan can be very useful in carrying out charitable intentions. A bequest can be a specific dollar amount, a percentage of an estate, or a percentage of the residual of an estate. A bequest made through the Presbyterian Church (U.S.A.) Foundation can be used to establish a permanent fund for a favorite mission cause, to create a life-income plan for a loved one, or to make an outright gift.

All bequests to the national agencies, councils, former corporations, and constituent corporations of the Presbyterian Church (U.S.A.) Foundation, with the exception of bequests to the Board of Pensions, are accepted and administered by the Presbyterian Church (U.S.A.) Foundation and are listed as gifts to the Presbyterian Church (U.S.A.).

The Foundation has served the Presbyterian Church, its congregations, related institutions, and agencies since 1799. The Foundation is responsible for the management of over $1,800,000,000 and the administration of nearly 6,000 life-income plans and for providing wills and bequest programs for the denomination.

TYPES OF BEQUESTS

- *Steward Fund:* An irrevocable contribution in which the donor or his/her designees advise the Presbyterian Church (U.S.A.) Foundation on charitable distributions from the fund to benefit mission over a span of years. A gift to the Foundation for the fund must be absolute to qualify as a charitable contribution for tax purposes; that is, the donor's recommendations must be advisory only.

- *Life Insurance Policies:* The church or an organization that is part of the church may be named beneficiary of an existing policy or a newly purchased policy. Proceeds from such policies are usually exempt from taxes and, if the assignment of the policy is irrevocable, present values and future premiums may qualify as charitable contributions.

- *Permanent Funds:* An irrevocable perpetual endowment gift. The gift itself and any additional contributions are permanently held, invested, and reinvested by the Presbyterian Church (U.S.A.) Foundation. The donor establishes what is paid to the designated charitable beneficiary to further the mission of the church.

- *Charitable Lead Trust:* A trust in which the donor transfers property to a trust and allots the income interest in the property in favor of a congregation or ministry of the Presbyterian Church (U.S.A.) for a period of years or for the life or lives of an individual(s). The remainder interest is either retained by the donor or given to a noncharitable beneficiary, usually children or grandchildren. The charitable lead trust is used for charitable giving by individuals both during their lifetimes and in their estate plans. It is also used as part of a plan for transfer of the remainder to younger-generation family members.

DEFERRED GIVING PROGRAM BENEFITS

- Deferred giving allows donors more alternatives.

- Deferred giving creates irrevocable sources of funds for the future.

- After-tax benefits of a planned gift may enable a larger gift to the annual budget/capital campaign.

- Deferred giving builds relationships with donors who have made a significant long-term commitment.

SUMMARY

An intentional program of planned giving benefits the church and the donor. It is the intelligent structuring of a person's financial affairs that benefits self, family, and charitable institutions. Planned giving does this by reducing taxes, increasing current income, and providing an effective and efficient means of increasing our ability to share and give to the church.

Planned giving programs educate church members about two areas:

- They can afford to give.

- They cannot afford not to plan.

The main components of good estate planning are preserving assets during our lifetime by properly titling assets to take advantage of probate and tax laws so that we may minimize taxes, plan tax-smart IRA distributions, or plan for incompetencies. The church's planned giving committee can make suggestions to assist members in obtaining in-depth information. We need to progress past the myths and horror stories that hold us hostage so that as the charitable pie is sliced thinner, a stable source of funding is available that extends stewardship beyond a human lifetime.

The Presbyterian Foundation makes the following resources available at no cost:

Wills Emphasis Leadership Guide
Foundation Planning Calendar and Workbook
Endowments: A Vision for Any Mission
Giving That Gives Back

Find more helpful resources by calling The Presbyterian Church (U.S.A.) Foundation at 1-800-858-6127.

QUESTIONS FOR THOUGHT AND DISCUSSION

1. What are the strengths of your current planned giving program?

2. What information in the previous chapters could be incorporated in your planned giving program to build on the strengths above?

Chapter 9

ENDOWMENT FUNDS

The universal human yearning (is) for something
permanent, enduring, without shadow of change.
Willa Cather

The unrelenting nature of change and the impermanence of life create in people the hope that they can leave a tangible legacy to satisfy the universal yearning for permanence. An endowment is a permanent fund—a mandate—to safeguard the future mission of a church. Endowments are scarce, rare resources that are not earned, not deserved. They exist because God is bountiful and has instilled a sense of vision in the generous among us. Simply put, endowment funds are a pool of money set aside to fund mission, program, or capital needs.

An endowment should enrich the witness of a church into the future. When times of demographic change or economic upheaval strike a community, an endowment can bridge the gap and allow churches to continue their outreach ministries while securing or retaining capable leadership.

An endowment is a joint venture that allows us to be a partner with God long after we are gone from this world. It should set forth the vision of the congregation for the future by tying it to the history and roots of the church and to its current ministry in the community and the world. Leadership, trust, involvement, accountability, and communication are the cornerstones of a successful endowment program. They require intentional activity today to make a difference tomorrow.

Because the principal is kept intact and invested, a predictable source of income allows a session to make creative, courageous, multi-year commitments. The purpose is not to perpetuate an institution, to memorialize the past, or to build a cold monument, but to establish a firm financial base so that the great commission can be fulfilled.

EMOTIONS AND ENDOWMENTS

Just as we have chronically conflicted emotions about our personal wealth, we bring these same sorts of problems into the church as we deal with corporate wealth. If we build an endowment, does it mean that we are cheating mission now? Are we holding onto outdated priorities? Do we no longer trust God to provide? We must have positive, creative leadership to move beyond an income-oriented view of funding mission. The objective of the Endowment Committee is to create the vision and the framework so that endowments are viewed as a sacred trusts for the future, not a reason to limit current gifts.

THEOLOGY AND ENDOWMENTS

Some theological principles can assist a church in reflecting on how to establish and use an endowment.

1. *How should we use an endowment?* Remember that an endowment is a special resource given by God and should be used for special purposes.

2. *Will an endowment tempt us to think that we have special (superior) ideas about how to serve God?* Remember that having been granted a special resource confers added responsibility, not religious authority.

3. *How can we use the endowment so that we become a blessing?*
   - Create projects that others won't undertake.
   - Take some risk by looking at multiyear funding of a new ministry.
   - Match congregational giving for mission.
   - Invest in the future.
   - Give beyond our own door.
   - Remember that the gifts God entrusts to us should not spoil us.

The pastor and session hold the key in establishing a program that will:

- Not detract from current giving
- Protect any donor restrictions
- Maintain confidentiality
- Encourage generosity

GIVING AND ENDOWMENTS

We are uneasy about congregations holding wealth and the impact that it may have on the annual giving of our members. There are both perils and potentials of congregational endowments. Recent research from the Alban Institute and the Lilly Foundation shows some patterns appearing:

1. A growing number of congregations have endowments in excess of $1,000,000.

2. An endowment does not adversely affect annual stewardship programs if there is:

   • A clear resolution and bylaws governing the acceptance and use of endowment funds

   • Regular full disclosure of all funds held by the congregation

   • Full reporting of the usage of the income from the endowment

   • Demonstrated prudent money management

3. Mission and ministry are visibly enriched because an endowment encourages members to consider bequests from their accumulated resources or the completion of a life-income plan.

CREATING AN ENDOWMENT

The Presbyterian Church (U.S.A.) Foundation supports the creation of endowment programs. The Foundation provides materials at no charge to assist pastors, sessions, and committees with the creation and maintenance of endowments. The Foundation also employs highly trained development officers who are available to assist sessions and individuals.

LEADERSHIP

Fears are often experienced that an endowment will hurt giving in the church. However, endowments do not exist in and of themselves. They are a created entity that draws life from the document that created it, the bylaws that govern it, and the leadership that sees to its management. Leadership makes the difference in this critical area of stewardship. Intentional, consistent, and strong pastoral and lay leadership is essential so that a congregation's endowment becomes a dynamic, vibrant, and fundamental part of our understanding of stewardship and not a crutch to support the annual budget.

THE RESOLUTION

Once the decision has been made to create or grow an endowment, a resolution needs to be drafted and approved by the session. The resolution should give the theological and ecclesiastical basis for an endowment as it relates to accumulated resources. The purpose for which the endowment income will be used needs to be clearly stated. A statement regarding how the endowment income will expand the mission and not diminish stewardship is helpful.

INVESTMENT POLICY

The investment goals and use of income and principal should be discussed. Any ethical guidelines about investments should be highlighted. Commitment to honor donor restrictions should be noted. It is important to avoid creating situations that put members in positions where their decisions create a conflict of interest. The kinds of gifts that will be accepted and the conditions under which gifts will be received, as well as the authority of the session to accept or reject gifts, belong in this section of a resolution.

Administration procedures would include such items as:

- Amendment procedures
- Accounting procedures
- Annual audit reports
- Legal work

MANAGING THE ENDOWMENT

Once funds are received, a decision must be made about funds management. Most states have passed legislation regarding the management of endowments that requires a total return on investment philosophy. Many states now hold fiduciaries accountable under this standard of performance commonly referred to as the Prudent Investor Rule. The process is the measure by which fiduciaries are judged on the proper discharge of investment responsibility. As a consequence, asset allocation, money manager selection, conflicts of interest, and performance related to stated goals must be taken into account with reference to state law.

PUBLICIZING THE ENDOWMENT

The primary role of the Endowment Committee is education. Getting the word out about memorials, bequests, and life-income plans is the lifeblood of new funds in the endowment. The articulation of opportunities and possibilities through ongoing storytelling in sermons, committee and session meetings, newsletters, bulletin announcements, brochures, videotapes, special events, and one-to-one conversations are some of the possibilities.

The time for making gifts is often associated with life-changing events such as death, retirement planning, illness, marriage or remarriage, divorce, becoming an empty nester, or a capital campaign. Because these event-related gifts require someone saying the right thing and listening for the right clues, the committee, pastor, and advisory group all need to be trained.

The committee should start with a written multiyear plan that includes the development of a core group of volunteers. The plan should include the evaluation of the program. Other steps include doing a survey to determine who has completed a planned gift, creating a maintenance function, and consulting with other stewardship committees. The development staff of the Presbyterian Church (U.S.A.) Foundation is an invaluable resource of ideas and materials, which are provided at no charge.

RECOGNITION SOCIETY

The willingness to provide information, to manage funds well, to have transparent account-ability in the receiving and administering of gifts sets the stage for the final component of an endowment program. Appropriate thanksgiving and public acknowledgment of gifts in the context of good stewardship lead to more gifts. It is important to say "thank you" in tasteful ways that allow us to celebrate our common values and challenge each person to consider all that God has done.

QUESTIONS FOR THOUGHT AND DISCUSSION

1. What are the strengths of your current endowment programs?

2. What information in the previous chapters could be incorporated in your endowment program to build on the strengths above?

Chapter 10

A CASE STUDY

The purpose of this case study is to provide the story of a congregation whose approach to stewardship developed, using all the steps in previous chapters, into a comprehensive plan that increased the participation and giving level of members and friends.

This case study will be useful to you and the Stewardship, Finance, and Planned Giving Committees as you plan your stewardship emphasis. To get the most benefit from the case study, follow these suggested guidelines:

1. Read about Knox-Calvin Presbyterian Church and underline the activities and plans described that are going well in your congregation's stewardship emphasis. Make a list of these.

2. Underline twice the activities and plans described that need to be strengthened in your congregation's stewardship emphasis. Make a list of these.

3. Circle the activities and plans that are not happening in your congregation. Make a list of these

4. Share your individual lists with the other members of your committee. Select two items to be continued, two items to be strengthened, and two items to be added from each of the three combined lists.

5. Plan a time for all related committees to share their lists.

6. Determine which members on the committees have a passion for working on these items and formulate a plan of action and change.

AN IDEAL CHURCH PROGRAM:
KNOX-CALVIN PRESBYTERIAN CHURCH

Knox-Calvin Presbyterian Church is a congregation in a suburban setting. The membership is 350; the average worship attendance is 215, and the church has 175 giving households. The congregation was organized in 1963 and has experienced slow, steady growth in membership and giving.

The church has a mission-based narrative budget that is presented to the congregation as a vision for outreach. It does a capital campaign every five years for capital needs, program, endowment, and mission. It has a Wills Emphasis Sunday annually. It participates in all four special offerings of the Presbyterian Church (U.S.A.).

Its committee structure dealing with stewardship is made up of a finance committee, mission interpretation committee, stewardship committee, and planned giving/endowment committee. Each is an independent session committee, but together they co-ordinate the year-round stewardship activities of the congregation with one another.

The pastor is intimately involved in the stewardship program of the church and enthusiastically supports the efforts of the committees. There is a solid attitude of teamwork with the pastor and committees combining their efforts in all aspects of the plan.

The church has not always been this well organized or well coordinated in its financial giving. Life has changed a great deal in the last five years.

FIVE YEARS AGO

- There were 125 giving households.

- There was no mission statement or "commonly acknowledged, overarching vision."

- The pastor preached only one stewardship sermon.

- There was one committee for finance and stewardship, and all members were from the Civic Generation. And it was difficult to find new members.

- This committee hastily planned a three-week giving emphasis for the annual giving campaign.

- A letter was mailed to giving households asking for pledges.

- Per capita giving was $752, yielding an annual budget of $94,000.

- The amount pledged that year was lower than the year before.

- This was the second year in a row that pledges were less.

- Only 50 percent of the giving households pledged.

- Although this congregation prided itself in being a mission-minded congregation, the missions budget was cut once again.

- Through the encouragement of the Presbyterian Women, the Christmas Joy Offering was received. It was the only special offering received.

FOUR YEARS AGO

- The pastor began preaching two stewardship sermons.

- The finance and stewardship committees were separated, and membership reflected the generational makeup of the congregation.

- Focus groups were formed to create a mission statement for future mission and ministry.

- A study was done in Generational theory and related giving patterns.

- Christmas Joy and One Great Hour of Sharing were received.

- Members of the finance and the stewardship committees attended workshops sponsored by the presbytery.

- The pastor and session studied *Giving and Stewardship in an Effective Church* by Kennon Callahan.

THREE YEARS AGO

- A stewardship-planning calendar was developed to integrate the annual giving and planning giving campaigns.

- The church began receiving all four special Presbyterian Church (U.S.A.) offerings.

- A planned giving committee was formed to create an endowment resolution and begin a wills and bequests program.

- The pastor started preaching three stewardship sermons in the fall.

- The results of the focus groups were identified, and the mission/vision focus was shared.

- Attention was paid to appeals to different motivations for giving.

- The stewardship committee researched various annual giving campaigns, selected one that was most appropriate for the congregation, and began planning.

- Results from the generational study were reported, and the information was used in shaping the stewardship emphasis.

- Members of the three committees participated in an event sponsored by the presbytery.

Two Years Ago

- Members of the three committees participated in an event sponsored by the Presbyterian Church (U.S.A.) Foundation and also attended the meeting of the PEER Network, a meeting of clergy and lay people concerned about endowments.

- The chair of the stewardship committee was asked to teach at the event sponsored by the Presbytery.

- Wills Emphasis Sunday was celebrated.

- The two-year promotional plan for planned giving was approved.

- The pastor preached stewardship sermons once a quarter.

- Small groups began a stewardship-related study.

- An adult church school class used the denominationally produced video, *The Stewardship of All Life,* as a basis for a study.

- The youth studied the resource "Choices."

Now

- The pastor preaches at least six stewardship sermons throughout the year.

- Everyone on the session and the financial related committees participates in small study groups to help members identify their own location in the generational constellation and to understand their money personality.

- These leaders identify the generations present in their congregation and organize the stewardship plan to allow for messages designed for different generations.

- There is a finance committee overseeing the spending process in the congregation.

- There is a stewardship committee overseeing the giving process in the congregation.

- There is a planned giving committee that coordinates with the finance and stewardship committees to encourage bequests.

- An endowment fund is being created.

- Members of all committees related to finance and stewardship participate in the presbytery-sponsored training events.

- The congregation is learning to share stories about the life of the church, the outreach activities, the mission of the presbytery, and General Assembly.

- At the training events, the committee members learn the importance of such things as saying thank you, communicating needs, etc.

- The four Presbyterian Church (U.S.A.) offerings continue to grow.

Chapter 11

LONG-RANGE PLANNING

The best fruits are plucked by each by some hand that is not [his] own.

C. S. Lewis

The development of a long-range financial plan for a congregation must be tied to the development and continual updating of the overall long-range plan. There are seven significant factors to consider in any long-range plan:

1. A financial long-range plan must be closely linked with the mission of the congregation. Be clear about the mission direction of a congregation, and building up the financial support will be easier.

2. Many leaders of a congregation should be part of developing the plan.

3. The plan must be written down.

4. Each part of the overall plan must take financial needs into consideration in a way that is realistic but not constrictive.

5. The plan must be at least three years and no more than four years long.

6. It must be evaluated and adjusted each year. This evaluation helps people celebrate what has been accomplished, and the adjustment allows for plans for the upcoming years to get more detailed as the time approaches.

7. It must be communicated to the congregation in exciting ways that encourage people to increase their giving to the annual budget and to develop expectations for planned giving.

One excellent way of beginning a long-range plan is to have key leaders, at least ten percent of your average worshiping congregation, work together on the Twelve Keys

planning process as identified in *Twelve Keys to An Effective Church,* by Kennon Callahan. This process helps a congregation identify its strengths and plan ways to build on
those strengths. The plan, built around the mission of the congregation, is developed
for a three-year period. There is much detail about the plans for the upcoming year,
less for the next year, and just rough ideas for the third year.

Each part of the overall long-range plan must contain information about the people and financial resources necessary to accomplish the objective established. The
planning work should be done in ways that are realistic but not discouraging. It is
helpful to continue to focus on the lives that will be affected and changed by this
mission objective. Talk about the negative impact as the cost of not reaching this
objective.

Every year at about the same time, the key leaders should meet to evaluate the
accomplishments for the current year, complete the plans for the next year, add more
details to the third year, and add another year with sketchy plans. The following are
questions to ask to help determine a multiyear or long-range budget. Also provided
are sample costs to guide you as you begin to assess a new mission project.

YEAR 1

1. **What is the cost of our current mission projects?**
   Current costs to underwrite the preschool; fund the parish nursing
   program; partial support for a Habitat for Humanity house construction;
   and mission giving to the presbytery, synod, and General Assembly
   by the congregation $ 67,500

2. **What is the remainder of the current year budget?**
   Remainder of current year budget $158,345

3. **What are the total costs for Year 1?** $225,854

YEAR 2

1. **What is the cost of current mission projects? (5 percent increase over Year 1)**
   Current costs to underwrite the preschool; fund the parish nursing
   program; partial support for a Habitat for Humanity house construction;
   and mission giving to the presbytery, synod, and General Assembly
   by the congregation $70,500

2. **What is the cost of new projects for Year 2?**
   New project—Cost of moving preschool to a 5-day-a-week program $30,000

3. **What is the estimated cost of future year's budget? (5 percent increase over
   Year 1)**
   Estimated cost of remainder of budget $166,000

4. **What are the total costs for Year 2?** $266,500

YEAR 3

1. **What is the cost of current mission projects? (5 percent increase over Year 2)**
   Current costs for the preschool 5 days a week; fund the parish nursing program; partial support for a Habitat for Humanity house construction; and mission giving to the presbytery, synod, and General Assembly by the congregation $81,500

2. **What is the cost of the projects for Year 3?**
   Cost of moving the preschool to a 12-hour day care center $43,000

3. **What is the estimated cost of future year's budget? (5 percent increase over Year 2)**
   Estimated cost of remainder of the budget $174,300

4. **What are the total costs for Year 3?** $298,800

YEAR 4

1. **What is the cost of current mission projects? (5 percent increase over Year 3)**
   Current costs for the day care center; fund the parish nursing program; partial support for a Habitat for Humanity house construction; and mission giving to the presbytery, synod, and General Assembly by the congregation $85,750

2. **What is the cost of projects for Years 4–5?**
   Continued improvement of the building and the outdoor play area; increasing the time for the parish nurse; extra support for the presbytery capital fund drive for a new church development $45,000

3. **What is the estimated cost of future year's budget? (5 percent increase over year 3)**
   Estimated cost of remainder of the budget $182,300

4. **What are total costs for Year 4?** $313,050

THE TOOLBOX

TOOL #1

GIVING IN YOUR CONGREGATION

A Matrix of History and Projections

INCOME SOURCES	3 years ago	2 years ago	1 year ago	Current year	1 year from now	2 years from now	3 years from now	4 years from now
Annual giving								
Investment income								
Endowments								
Capital campaigns								
Funds designated by giver								
Total income								
USE OF FUNDS								
Mission outside the church								
Operating expenses								
% Mission/ Operating								
Capital expenditures								
Total spending								
Difference								

ANNUAL GIVING	3 years ago	2 years ago	1 year ago	Current year	1 year from now	2 years from now	3 years from now	4 years from now
# Members								
Potential giving units								
Pledge units								
Total amount pledged								
Amount paid on pledges								
% pay-up								
Loose plate offering								
Bequests								
PC (USA) special offering*								
Designated giving								
Total giving								
Per member giving								
Per member giving as % of total								

* One Great Hour of Sharing, Pentecost, Peacemaking, Christmas Joy

ENDOWMENTS	3 years ago	2 years ago	1 year ago	Current year	1 year from now	2 years from now	3 years from now	4 years from now
Opening balance								
Additions to endowments								
New endowments								
Designated endowment expenditure								
Endowment funds closing balance								
Funds income earned								
Funds income percentage								
Fund income applied to current uses								
% fund income applied to current uses								
Fund growth amount								
Fund growth percentage								

MISSION GIVING	3 years ago	2 years ago	1 year ago	Current year	1 year from now	2 years from now	3 years from now	4 years from now
Presbytery, Synod, and General Assembly								
Per capita								
Designated giving PC (USA)								
Theological education fund—1 percent of mission budget								
Local mission								
Total PC (USA) mission giving								
Nonlocal mission unrelated to PC (USA)								
Total of all mission giving								
Mission % of total income								
Mission giving per giving unit								

TOOL #2

GIVING IN YOUR CONGREGATION BY GIVING UNITS

This chart gives an overview of giving patterns and is helpful in developing a strategy to increase the level of giving.

Giving units	3 years ago	2 years ago	1 year ago	Current year	1 year from now	2 years from now	3 years from now	4 years from now
$10,000+								
$5,000–$10,000								
$4,000–$4,999								
$3,000–$3,999								
$2,000–$2,999								
$1,000–$1,999								
$500–$999								
$250–$499								
$1–$249								
$0								

TOOL #3

CONGREGATIONAL ATTITUDES TOWARD MONEY AND GIVING

Conventional wisdom suggests that 20% of the people give 80% of the budget. The other 80% of the congregation sees that the bills are regularly paid without much effort from them, so why would they respond to a call for increased stewardship? *Behind the Stained Glass Windows,* p. 220

Therefore, for a congregation to increase its level of giving, attitudes toward money and giving need to be assessed. Barriers, congregational norms, and perceived realities must be acknowledged and discussed.

Select the number that most accurately reflects your opinion of your congregation's attitude toward money and giving in these areas.

Congregational personality described as	Worldly 1	2	3	4	Spiritual 5
Congregational Vision articulation . . .	Vague 1	2	3	4	Clear 5
Teaching/preaching on giving happens . . .	A little 1	2	3	4	A lot 5
Annual giving activities/ programs planning is . . .	Casual 1	2	3	4	Intentional 5
Giving plan targeted for new givers is . . .	Exclusive 1	2	3	4	Inclusive 5
Attitudes concerning money are . . .	Secretive 1	2	3	4	Open 5
Should pastors know giving levels . . .	No 1	2	3	4	Yes 5
Emphasis on managing money is . . .	A little 1	2	3	4	A lot 5
Emphasis on expanded giving is . . .	A little 1	2	3	4	A lot 5
Planned giving program is . . .	Casual 1	2	3	4	Intentional 5
Flow of church funds is . . .	Inward 1	2	3	4	Outward 5

To assess your attitude about money and giving, record the numbers in each category.

Congregational personality   _____

Congregational vision   _____

Teaching/preaching about giving   _____

Activities/programs about giving   _____

Giving plan targeted   _____

Attitudes concerning money   _____

Pastor knows giving level   _____

Emphasis on managing money   _____

Emphasis on expanded giving   _____

Planned giving program   _____

Flow of funds   _____

1. Discuss what you have learned about areas such as openness about money, intentionality of plans, and clarity of vision.

2. What changes should be planned to increase the level of giving in your congregation?

This tool can be used with a variety of groups such as the session, church school classes, givers to the church, nongivers to the church.

TOOL #4

MISSION-BASED BUDGET NARRATIVE

INVESTMENT LINE ITEM BUDGET

MISSION PRIORITIES

LINE ITEMS	$$	Ministry with children and their families	Corporate dynamic worship	Developing relational groups	Reaching out to the community	Pastoral care of members and friends	Increasing connection with other Presbyterians
MISSION							
• Churchwide mission	$112,000						$112,000
• Theological education	6,300						6,300
• Local mission	32,600	2,000	2,000	1,150	21,000		6,450
• Per capita	6,450						6,450
MUSIC	4,200		4,200				
CHRISTIAN EDUCATION							
• Children	8,560	8,560					
• Youth	12,000			10,000	2,000		
• Adults	4,500	3,300		1,200			
FACILITIES							
• Utilities	19,500	4,500	7,000	3,500	3,000	1,000	500
• Repairs	20,000	4,000	6,000	4,000	5,000	1,000	
• Services	18,000	5,400	5,600	4,000	2,000	1,000	
• Capital reserve	20,000	6,000	8,000		6,000		
• Insurance	9,000	3,000	3,000		2,000	1,000	
OFFICE EQUIPMENT POSTAGE, SUPPLIES	24,000	6,000	8,000	3,000	5,500	1,000	500
SALARIES AND BENEFITS							
• Pastor	$73,450	12,000	21,500	8,450	24,000	7,000	500
• Associate pastor	43,500	3,000	5,500	21,300	10,000	3,200	500
• Church educator	35,400	21,500	1,000	9,000	1,400	2,000	500
• Music staff	34,000	2,000	32,000				
• Office staff	62,500	13,300	18,950	13,000	7,000	10,000	250
TOTALS	$545,960	$94,560	$122,750	$78,600	$88,900	$27,200	$133,950

MISSION-BASED BUDGET NARRATIVE WORKSHEET

MISSION PRIORITIES

INVESTMENT LINE ITEM BUDGET

$$

LINE ITEMS								
TOTALS								

TOOL #5

CHECKLIST FOR SETTING UP AN ENDOWMENT FUND

Indicate on the line provided by each step "yes" or "no."

_____ The session accepts the concept.

_____ Committee created to explore possibilities, gather information, and outline an endowment program.

_____ The session receives report and authorizes development of a resolution.

_____ The committee considers:

- Sample bylaws
- Helpful additional guidelines
- Consulting legal counsel
- Providing for annual audit and report
- Providing for ongoing committee

_____ The session receives and approves the report establishing the endowment fund.

_____ The committee now plans the educational program and process that will educate and involve the entire congregation in understanding the meaning and intention of the endowment fund.

_____ The education plan includes at least:

- Wills emphasis materials
- Deferred giving materials
- Promotional/educational pieces for bulletins, newsletter, displays
- Small group seminars/classes on deferred giving
- Endowment Sunday celebration
- Regular Minutes for Mission at worship
- Public recognition of gifts received
- Public recognition of income used for mission, building, etc.
- Regular use of Presbyterian Church (U.S.A.) Foundation printed materials and personnel
- End of year gifts
- Repeat all of the above at least annually
- A calendar timeline for promoting endowment on an annual basis
- A *Book of Remembrance* memorializing donors
- Developing unique brochure for your church to promote endowment
- Itinerant speakers from mission causes benefiting from endowment
- Endowment-related educational topics included in annual planning

_____ The session and Endowment Committee will need to provide an investment policy for the endowment fund.

TOOL #6

A TWO-YEAR PROMOTIONAL PLAN FOR YOUR
CONGREGATION'S ENDOWMENT

MONTHS 1 TO 6 (SUMMER/FALL)

1. Create a brochure.

   - This could be a general piece using some of the information that is provided within the Presbyterian Church (U.S.A.) Foundation literature. Samples of other congregational endowment brochures are available from your Foundation representative.
   - The first brochure could simply be a bulletin insert.
   - If the bulletin insert style is used, a general brochure should still be created.

2. Distribute the general brochure.

   - Place it on literature tables and in pew racks.
   - Consider sending it in a newsletter annually.
   - Request visiting stewards to deliver it during the annual stewardship drive.
   - Include in a New Members Information Packet.

MONTHS 7 TO 12 (WINTER/SPRING)

1. Observe a Wills/Endowment Sunday that may include:

   - The congregations's general endowment brochure
   - Promotional materials from the Presbyterian Church (U.S.A.) Foundation
   - Posters
   - Bulletin inserts (printed or customized)
   - Newsletter and minute for mission copy
   - An adult Christian education program
   - A minute for mission explaining the church's endowment
   - A related sermon

MONTHS 13 TO 18 (SUMMER/FALL)

1. Conduct a special program or series of programs that include subjects such as:

   - Wills and trusts
   - Charitable estate planning
   - Advance directives
   - Living wills
   - Durable powers of attorney (health care, finances, etc.)

MONTHS 18 TO 24 (WINTER/SPRING)

1. Observe a second Wills/Endowment Sunday. (A Wills/Endowment Sunday should now be a natural part of your congregations's life. Observe it annually.)
2. Consider offering special programs that target certain groups in the congregation:

- A luncheon outlining the benefits of charitable life-income plans to be attended by attorneys, accountants, tax preparers
- A Wills and Estate-Planning Workshop for those aged 55+
- A Vacation Bible school built on a theme of stewardship such as "Nurturing Younger Stewards"

OTHER IDEAS . . .

- Conduct a Wills and Charitable Estate-Planning Workshop every other year.
- Prepare four 2–3 sentence paragraphs that the church secretary can "plug" into the newsletter.
- Highlight significant gifts (when permitted) in the newsletter.
- Prepare one sentence "blips" for the bulletin. Use these when the newsletter isn't issued that week.

TOOL #7

MONEY ATTITUDES INVENTORY

SECTION I.

Below is a list of 29 values. After reading the list, rank the values on a scale of 1 to 3 (most to least important). There is no right or wrong answer. The results are an aid to show how you feel about the values that guide your life. Several blanks are included should you wish to include other values.

_____	big investment portfolio
_____	comfortable life for self and family
_____	new home
_____	second home
_____	sense of accomplishment
_____	community service
_____	attending concerts, lectures, etc.
_____	education/personal enrichment
_____	excitement/adventure
_____	travel
_____	family activities
_____	family responsibilities
_____	health/fitness
_____	image
_____	personal appearance
_____	job success/advancement
_____	large salary
_____	prestige status
_____	free time/recreation
_____	eliminating debt
_____	saving
_____	tithing
_____	security
_____	shopping
_____	budgeting
_____	starting own business
_____	charitable contributions
_____	contentment
_____	mission trip
_____	_____
_____	_____

SECTION II.

This section helps you determine your attitudes about money. Honesty in answering these questions is key. Share your answers with the others in your group.

- Do you consider yourself a spender or a saver?

  _____

  _____

- Do you prefer to risk return, safety, or opportunity in your investment?

  _____

  _____

- Do you put off making decisions?

  _____

  _____

- Are you willing to lose some of your money? How much?

  _____

  _____

- Do you invest in fads?

  _____

  _____

- Are you willing to have debt and, if yes, what kind of debt (home, car, credit cards)?

  _____

  _____

- What type of investments do you have?

  _____

  _____

- Are you comfortable with your investments?

  _____

  _____

- Do you feel positive about the future financially?

  _____

  _____

- Is everything negotiable? What is not?

  _____

  _____

- How does money make you feel? Powerful? Anxious? Guilty?

  _____

  _____

SECTION III.

This section is designed to foster small group discussions about values, how you spend your money and your time, and the mission and ministry of the church. These topics can help break the silence surrounding money.

- Evaluate where you are spending your income. Do your investments and spending reflect how you view yourself? How others view you?

  _____

  _____

  _____

  _____

- Would anyone who looked through your checkbook or estate documents guess you were a Christian?

  _____

  _____

  _____

  _____

- What is poverty? Wealth? Where do you fit?

  _____

  _____

  _____

  _____

- What experiences have influenced your attitudes toward money?

  _____

  _____

  _____

  _____

TOOL #8

SCRIPTURE TEXTS FOR STEWARDSHIP

OLD TESTAMENT REFERENCES

Exodus 36:2–7	The people bring more than enough offerings (helpful for beginning a capital campaign)
Deuteronomy 26:1–15	Giving the first fruits
Psalm 24	The earth is the Lord's
Psalm 48:12–14	Telling the whole generation (Wills Emphasis)
Malachi 3:1–10	Tithing

NEW TESTAMENT REFERENCES

Matthew 6:25–34	"Seek first the kingdom of God"
Matthew 13:44–45	The parable of the treasure and the pearl
Matthew 15:32–38; Mark 8:1–9; Luke 9:12–17; John 6:1–14	Feeding of the 5,000
Matthew 19:23–30	"We have left all and followed you"
Matthew 25:14–30	The parable of the talents
Mark 12:13–17	Giving God the things that are God's
Mark 12:41–44	The widow's mite
Luke 11:1–10	The parable of the neighbor at midnight
Luke 11:42	Tithing
Luke 12:13–21	The parable of the rich fool
Luke 16:1–8	The parable of the unjust steward
Luke 18:18–30	The rich young ruler
1 Corinthians 16:1–4	"On the first day of the week"
2 Corinthians 8:8–15	Give according to what you have
2 Corinthians 9:6–15	"God loves a cheerful giver"
1 Peter 4:10–11	"Be good stewards of God's varied grace"

A more complete list of scripture references can be found in *A Stewardship Tour of the Bible* by Al Winn; PDS 918-86-310

TOOL #9

SPECTRUM ANALYSIS OF THE PASTOR'S ROLE IN STEWARDSHIP

Total laissez faire "It's none of my business" — A little preaching on the subject — Advise the stewardship committee but don't get too involved — If you fall somewhere in the middle you describe it — Promote financial stewardship at every opportunity — Demand a tithe and buttonhole wealthy individuals for specific contributions

1. Mark an "x" on this spectrum to indicate the role of your pastor in the stewardship program/emphasis/plans of your congregation.

2. Discuss with the pastor and members of the committees related to finance, stewardship and/or planned giving any desire for change.

3. Brainstorm strategies for change.

TOOL #10

FACTORS THAT DETERMINE OUR GIVING TO THE CHURCH

Rank the following statements 1 through 9, 1 being the most important and 9 being the least important, as factors that determine your giving to the church.

_____ past patterns of giving

_____ need of the church as an institution locally and beyond the local church

_____ what we have left after taxes, necessities, recreation

_____ biblical admonitions

_____ gratitude to God for God's goodness

_____ persuasiveness of the Stewardship Committee

_____ guilt

_____ love for those God loves and for whom the church ministers

_____ to reduce taxable income

What does this ranking say to the Stewardship Committee and its job and approach?

TOOL #11

IMPORTANT ADDRESSES

Presbyterian Endowment Education and Resource Network
807 West 32nd Street
Wilmington, DE 19802
302–764–8782
www.peernetwork.org

Presbyterian Church (U.S.A.) Investment and Loan Program, Inc.
100 Witherspoon Street
Louisville, KY 40202
1–800–903–7457
Fax: 502–569–8868

Office of Stewardship
Presbyterian Church (U.S.A.)
100 Witherspoon Street
Louisville, KY 40202
1–888–728–7228, ex. 5164
502–569–5123
www.pcusa.org
Fax: 502–569–8060

Presbyterian Church (U.S.A.) Foundation
200 East 12th Street
Jeffersonville, IN 47130
1–800–858–6127
www.fdn.pcusa.org
Fax: 502–284–5664   (Marketing and Development)
Fax: 502–569–5980

Church Financial Campaign Service
Presbyterian Church (U.S.A.)
100 Witherspoon St.
Louisville, KY 40202
1–888–219–6513
www.pcusa.org
Fax: 502–569–8884

TOOL #12

THE TWELVE STRENGTHS OF STEWARDSHIP

This song is sung to the traditional tune of
"The Twelve Days of Christmas"
The words are by Jim Barnett, Development Officer,
The Presbyterian Church (U.S.A.) Foundation

Oh the *first* strength of stewardship is easy for you to see
A clear call to mission in the world.

Oh the *second* strength of stewardship is easy for you to see
Free willingness and
A clear call to mission in the world.

Oh the *third* strength of stewardship is easy for you to see
Too much love, Free willingness, and
A clear call to mission in the world.

Oh the *fourth* strength of stewardship is easy for you to see
Foretold budget, Too much love, Free willingness, and
A clear call to mission in the world.

Oh the *fifth* strength of stewardship is easy for you to see
Live leadership, Foretold budget, Too much love, Free willingness, and
A clear call to mission in the world.

Oh the *sixth* strength of stewardship is easy for you to see
Six months of planning, Live leadership,
Foretold budget, Too much love, Free willingness, and
A clear call to mission in the world.

Oh the *seventh* strength of stewardship is easy for you to see
Seven committee meetings, Six months of planning, Live leadership,
Foretold budget, Too much love, Free willingness, and
A clear call to mission in the world.

Oh the *eighth* strength of stewardship is easy for you to see
Eight Stewardship minutes, Seven committee meetings, Six months of planning, Live leadership,
Foretold budget, Too much love, Free willingness, and
A clear call to mission in the world.

Oh the *ninth* strength of stewardship is easy for you to see
Ninety-nine percent coverage, Eight stewardship minutes, Seven committee meetings,
Six months of planning, Live leadership, Foretold budget, Too much love, Free willingness, and
A clear call to mission in the world.

Oh the *tenth* strength of stewardship is easy for you to see
Ten times the faith, Ninety-nine percent coverage, Eight stewardship minutes,
Seven committee meetings, Six months of planning, Live leadership,
Foretold budget, Too much love, Free willingness, and
A clear call to mission in the world.

Oh the *'leventh* strength of stewardship is easy for you to see
Leavening of the church, Ten times the faith, Ninety-nine percent coverage,
Eight Stewardship minutes, Seven committee meetings, Six months of planning, Live leadership,
Foretold budget, Too much love, Free willingness, and
A clear call to mission in the world.

Oh the *twelfth* strength of stewardship is easy for you to see
Wealth of information, Leavening of the church, Ten times the faith,
Ninety-nine percent coverage, Eight stewardship minutes, Seven committee meetings,
Six months of planning, Live leadership, Foretold budget, Too much love, Free willingness, and
A clear call to mission in the world.

TOOL #13

COMPUTER PROGRAMS THAT ARE HELPFUL

There are a number of fully integrated church software programs available to maintain church records, which include:

- Membership modules that maintain information on membership that allows you to print directories, mailing labels, and lists.

- Accounting programs that are specifically designed for church record keeping make it easier to do the business of the church. Minimum requirements for accounting would include General Ledger, Accounts Payable, and Receipts (Contributions or Gifts) modules.

- The Contributions or Gifts modules enable the recording of member pledges and giving. They also generate monthly, quarterly, and/or annual statements. The reports generated can be a resource for seasonal budget planning.

Many packages offer modules to record attendance and participation of members as well as financial information.

Fixed assets can be tracked, and sermon writing is an option with some.

Some programs that are available are:

- ACS, Automated Church Systems

- Shelby Systems

- Church Windows

- Shepherds Staff

- Ease

- Power Church

The cost of these programs varies. In many cases, you can begin with Membership, Contributions and Gifts, and the General Ledger to get started, then add additional modules to track and maintain additional records.

STEWARDSHIP RESOURCES

** Indicates books cited in this book. The other publications are helpful and practical.

** Bassler, Jouette M, *God and Mammon—Asking for Money in the New Testament* (Nashville: Abingdon Press, 1991).

** Callahan, Kennon, *Effective Church Finances* (San Francisco: Jossey-Bass, 1996).

** Callahan, Kennon, *Giving and Stewardship in an Effective Church* (San Francisco: Jossey-Bass, 1996).

** Callahan, Kennon, *Twelve Keys to an Effective Church* (San Francisco: Jossey-Bass, 1996).

** "Choices: Living and Learning in God's World" (Louisville, Ky.: Stewardship Education Team, Presbyterian Church [U.S.A.], 1997).

Condon, Gerald, and Jeffrey Condon, *Beyond the Grave; The Right Way and the Wrong Way of Leaving Money to Your Children (and Others)* (New York: Harper Business, 1996).

** The Four Churchwide Special Offerings of the Presbyterian Church (U.S.A.) (Louisville, Ky.: Mission Interpretation and Promotion, 1997).

** Gast, Aaron E., Endowments: A Biblical Base (Jeffersonville, Ind.: Presbyterian (U.S.A.) Foundation, 1988).

** Hall, Douglas John, *The Steward—A Biblical Symbol Come of Age* (New York: Friendship Press, 1982).

Hoge, Dean R., Benton Johnson, and Donald A. Luidens, *Vanishing Boundaries: The Religion of Mainline Protestant Baby Boomers* (Louisville, Ky.: Westminster/John Knox, 1994).

Hoge, Dean, Charles Zech, and Patrick McNamara, *Plain Talk about Churches and Money* (Bethesda, Md.: Alban Institute, 1997).

** Hoge, Dean, Charles Zech, Patrick McNamara, and Michael Donahue, *Money Matters: Personal Giving in American Churches* (Louisville, Ky.: Westminster/John Knox, 1996).

** Hudnut-Beumler, James, "Creating a Commonwealth: The Theology and Ethics of Church Endowments," *Congregation* (July–August 1997).

** Jordan, Ronald R., and Katelyn L. Quynn, *Planned Giving: Management, Marketing, and Law* (New York: John Wiley & Sons, Inc., 1995).

** Mead, Loren, *Endowed Congregations: Pros and Cons.* Alban Institute special paper. (Bethesda, Md.: Alban Institute, 1991).

** LeBow, Victor, "Price Competition in 1955." *Journal of Retailing* (Spring 1955): 7. Quoted in Vance Packard, *The Waste Makers* (New York: McKay, 1960), 24.

Needleman, Jacob, *Money and the Meaning of Life* (New York: Doubleday, 1994).

** Nichols, Judith, *Targeted Fund Raising* (Chicago: Precept Press, 1996).

** Nouwen, Henri, *Circles of Love* (London: Darton, Longman, & Todd, 1988).

** Owensby, Walter L., *Economics for Prophets* (Grand Rapids: Wm. B. Eerdmans Publishing Co., 1988).

** Philippe, William, *Creative Use of Endowment* (Jeffersonville, Ind.: Presbyterian (U.S.A.) Foundation, 1992).

Philippe, William, *A Stewardship Scrapbook* (Jeffersonville, Ind.: Presbyterian (U.S.A.) Foundation, 1999).

Presbyterian Program Planning Calendar, (Louisville, Ky.: Mission Interpretation and Promotion, Presbyterian Church [U.S.A.], 2000).

** Prince, Russ Allen, and Karen Mary File, *The Seven Faces of Philanthropy* (San Francisco: Jossey-Bass, 1994).

Ronsvalle, John, and Silvia Ronsvalle, *At Ease: Discussing Money and Values in Small Groups* (Bethesda, Md.: Alban Institute, 1998).

** Ronsvalle, John, and Silvia Ronsvalle, *Behind the Stained Glass Windows–Money Dynamics in the Church* (Grand Rapids: Baker Books, 1996).

Stanley, Thomas J., and William D. Danko, *The Millionaire Next Door* (Marietta, Ga.: Longstreet, 1996).

** Strass, William, and Neil Howe, *Generations: The History of America's Future: 1584 to 2069* (New York: Quill, 1931).

** Strass, William, and Neil Howe, "The Cycle of Generations," *American Demographics* (April 1991): 24–34.

** *The Stewardship Manual* (Louisville, Ky.: Presbyterian Church [U.S.A.], 1994).

** Wheeler, Sondra Ely, *Wealth as Peril and Obligation: The New Testament on Possessions* (Grand Rapids: Wm. B. Eerdmans Publishing Co., 1995).

White, Douglas E., *The Art of Planned Giving: Understanding Donors and the Culture of Giving* (New York: John Wiley & Sons, Inc., 1995).

** Wuthnow, Robert, *God and Mammon in America* (New York: Free Press—A Division of Macmillan, Inc., 1994).

Wuthnow, Robert, *Poor Richard's Principle* (New Jersey: Princeton University Press, 1996).